RUGBY
Skills, Tactics and Rules

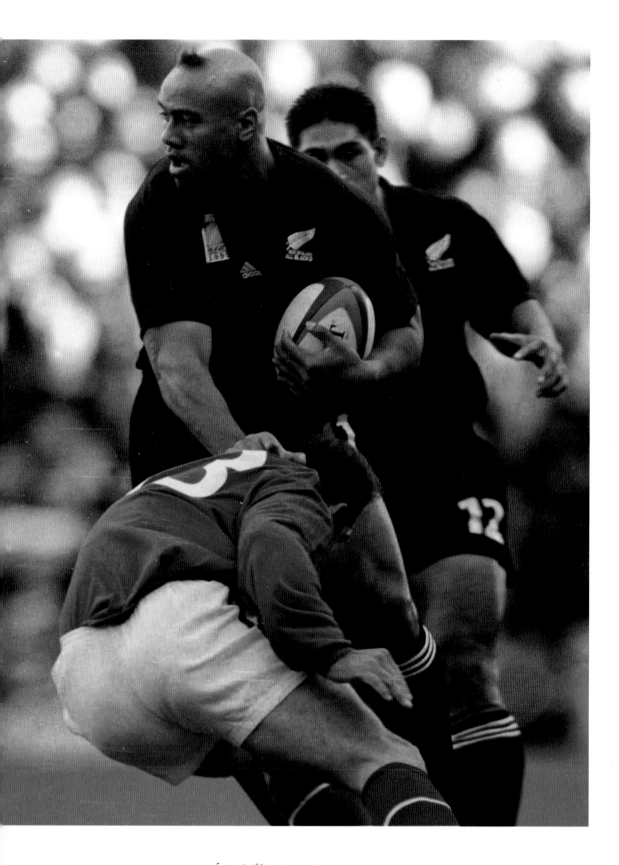

RUGBY
SKILLS, TACTICS
and RULES

TONY WILLIAMS
and
GORDON HUNTER

FIREFLY BOOKS

A FIREFLY BOOK

Published by Firefly Books Ltd. 2000

Copyright © 2000 Tony Williams and Gordon Hunter
Copyright © 2000 David Bateman Ltd.

First printing

**Library of Congress Cataloging in Publication Data
is available.**

Canadian Cataloguing in Publication Data

**Williams, Tony, 1960-
Rugby skills, tactics and rules**

**Includes index.
ISBN 1-55209-546-0**

1. Rugby football. I. Hunter, Gordon, 1949- . II. Title.

GV945.W54 2000   796.333'2   C00-930923-3

Published in Canada in 2000 by
Firefly Books Ltd.
3680 Victoria Park Avenue
Willowdale, Ontario
M2H 3K1

Published in the United States in 2000 by
Firefly Books (U.S.) Inc.
P.O.Box 1338, Ellicott Station
Buffalo, New York
14205

Photographs by Fotopress Limited, Auckland, New Zealand
Design by Chris O'Brien/Pages Literary Pursuits, Auckland
Printed in Hong Kong by Colorcraft

Half-title: Jonah Lomu knocks over Daniel Herbert on his way to the goal line.
Title page: Power, poise and purpose — Jonah Lomu.
Page 5: Christian Cullen accelerates through the gap.
Page 7: Tim Horan, player of the 1999 World Cup, in full flight against South Africa in the semi-final which Australia won 27-21.
Page 8: Full physical contact as a crunching tackle from Brian Lima causes Afato So'oalo to spill the ball. *Top:* A rugby player has to have the right attitude — concentration, aggression and commitment — as Kees Meeuws exemplifies here.
Page 9: The thrill of running with the ball is evident on the face of Philippe Bernat-Salles on his way to a try against Argentina in the World Cup. *Bottom:* Wellington's Tana Umaga is slowed down by Auckland's Doug Howlett, but not stopped.
Page 10: The satisfied smile of victory on the face of Owen Finigan after he scored one of the tries that won the 1999 World Cup for Australia. *Bottom:* Pita Alatini has tried in vain to slip through the gap.
Page 11: With so many players off their feet at the ruck, the referee must have been close to blowing his whistle before Argentina's Agustin Pichot figured out this dive pass.

Contents

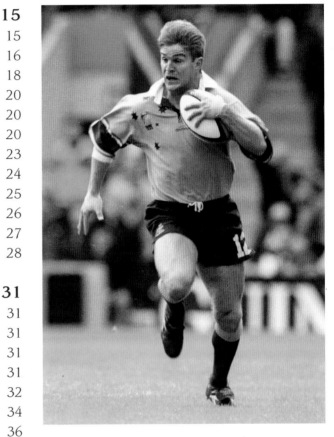

Introduction
The Game for all Shapes and Sizes

Pictured on the cover of this book is what many regard as the most thrilling sight in world rugby — the massive bulk of Jonah Lomu on the charge. But you don't have to be huge to play rugby. The reason it is the greatest game in the world is because anyone, regardless of weight or size, can play it; there is a place in a rugby team for all. It is also the most complete game. You can run with the ball or kick it; if your opponent has it, you can tackle him, push him, pull him, maul him — and it is all within the rules!

Rugby is a very physical game. It is also a thinking game with endless tactical variations which require a great many skills. This makes it a fascinating game both to play and to watch.

Rugby – Skills, Tactics and Rules is laid out in such a way that any player from the age of about 10 can learn the skills. It begins with an explanation of the individual skills from the most basic through to the specialised, followed by unit and team skills, moves and strategies, layered one on top of the other. Towards the back of the book is a plain language guide to the rules of rugby and a glossary so that rugby terms can be clearly understood.

Rugby – Skills, Tactics and Rules gives a formal framework for anyone wishing to learn the skills of rugby or to improve their existing skills, but it is only a framework. Players should learn to think for themselves and be innovative. Coaches, too, will find this book of immense value.

A would-be tackler bites the dust in the wake of Jonah Lomu on the charge.

1.

Rugby is a Team Game

The objective in rugby is to score more points than your opponents. This can be achieved by scoring tries, kicking goals or a combination of both. Scoring tries is the real joy of rugby. Though individuals score tries, rugby is a team game and every member of the team contributes in some way to the tries that are scored.

The team that takes the field consists of 15 people but up to seven 'extra' players can sit on the bench and be used as replacements during the game. These extra players are generally known as substitutes or reserves.

In the very early days of rugby the game was played with a pig's bladder and contested by whole villages in Europe. Some players would go *forward* to join the huge mass of bodies wrestling for the 'ball', while others would stay *back* ready to have a run with it when it came free. In this way the two basic positions in rugby, Forwards and Backs, were formed.

Nowadays, a rugby team (or 'XV' as it is often written) consists of eight forwards and seven backs. The forwards are usually subdivided into the front row (3), the second row (2) and the back row (3). The backs are referred to as the halves (2), the three-quarters (4) and the fullback.

The basics

Every player in a team has similar **individual skills**, such as passing and catching. The level of the passing skills should be high throughout the team, no matter what the position. This has become especially important today with the emphasis on retaining possession of the ball.

Good tight protection from his forwards allows Jacob Rauluni to kick Fiji back onto the attack.

The team has **unit skills**, such as the front row of the scrum pushing as a unit. There are **forward skills**, such as are required in scrums and lineouts, and **back skills**, such as speed and deception. Then there are **team skills** in which different units or individuals work with other units or individuals.

The highest level of skill and teamwork (and the most exciting) is called **open rugby** — when play moves about the field and players are often required to use the skills of players in other positions. A prop might have to kick the ball into touch; a wing might have to go into a maul and wrestle for the ball; a second-rower might have to sprint to the line to score a try. Players should always be alert, skilled and innovative.

The positions

The position in a rugby team tells a player where he stands on the field, how he fits into a team and what his duties are.

The names given to the fifteen different positions have changed over the years with regional variations also confusing the issue. In New Zealand, for example, the names given to the backs have been based on a system determined by their distance from the scrum: halves, five-eighths, centre, threequarters and fullback. In other parts of the world the halfback is usually called the scrum-half; the first five-eighth is known as the fly-half, outside-half or stand-off; the centres are the inside centre and the outside centre, and so on. The front row and the second row are together called

Coaches and teams should not get tied down by tradition — be innovative.

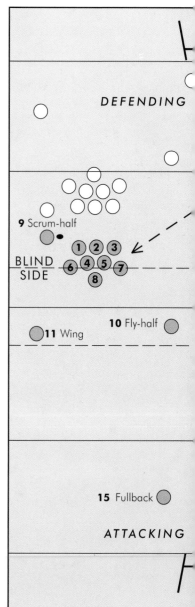

Above: The tackle from behind starts with the chase; Christian Cullen pursuing Scotland's Gary Armstrong.

Right: Rugby is a tough game. Tony Brown of the Otago Highlanders discovers his opponents not only want the ball, but also the shirt off his back.

Below: How they line up — the fifteen members of a team taking up their positions for a set scrum.

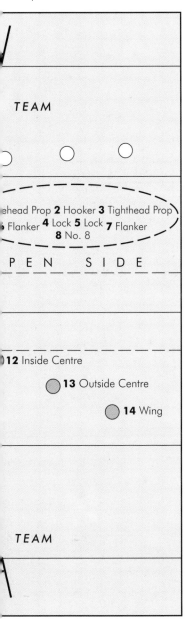

TEAM

○ ○ ○

ehead Prop **2** Hooker **3** Tighthead Prop
Flanker **4** Lock **5** Lock **7** Flanker
8 No. 8

P E N   S I D E

12 Inside Centre

● **13** Outside Centre

● **14** Wing

TEAM

the tight five; the flankers and No. 8 combined are often called the loose forwards or 'loosies'. But for the sake of consistency this book will use the terms which are generally understood throughout most of the rugby-playing world. These are shown in the diagram at left.

Basic skills required to pick an age-group team

Prop – the two most solid
Hooker – solid, good lineout thrower
Locks or Second row – the two tallest
Flankers – fittest
No. 8 – biggest and most skilful
Scrum-half – best long passer
Fly-half – best kicker
Centres – best passers
Wings – the two fastest
Fullback – best catcher of the high ball

17

Prop

The word prop means *to hold up* or *support* and that is what props do. (In France a prop is a *pilier* — a pillar.) The props support the hooker in a set scrum or a jumper at the lineout and at kick restarts. A prop needs strength and good technique.

There are two props, the loosehead prop (who wears the number 1 jersey) and the tighthead prop (number 3 jersey). The loosehead stands on the left side of the hooker, the side where his scrum-half puts the ball into the scrum. He is called the loosehead prop because when the scrum binds, his is the 'loose' (free) head on the outside of the scrum.

The loosehead's job is to make sure the hooker can get a good view of the ball when it is put in by his scrum-half. To do this he has to be able to keep the opposing prop from disrupting the scrum and obstructing the hooker's view.

The tighthead prop stands on the other side of the hooker. His

Above: A Canterbury Crusader prop has gone low, driven through the tackle and has a firm hold on the ball as he grounds it. Try!

Left: Prop Kees Meeuws of the Otago Highlanders carries out his duty, charging the ball forward in open play. Note his body position, ready to dip for the impact.

job is to keep the scrum firm and steady on his side's put-in, and to try to disrupt it when the opposition is putting the ball in.

Usually the props will stand at numbers one and three in the lineout to support the main jumpers, who usually stand at positions two and four. The props must protect the jumper from interference, assist his jump and protect the ball from the other team.

Because of their strength, props are often used to rip the ball free at mauls and to charge forward with the ball alongside rucks, mauls and lineouts.

Main skills: Scrummaging; supporting taller players at kick-offs and lineouts
Main practice: Strength training and scrummaging

Below: The English front row looks a solid unit ready for engagement.

Hooker

A hooker is a prop with specialised tasks. Not so long ago the primary task of a hooker was to use his feet to 'hook' back the ball in the set scrums in order to gain possession for his side. Though there are fewer scrums in modern rugby this is still the hooker's main role. If he is able to win the ball on his opponent's put-in, it is called striking 'against the head' or a 'tight head'.

These days the hooker is usually the player who throws in the ball at a lineout. He is also expected to be mobile, operating almost as a loose forward when the loosies have got tied up in a ruck or maul. Some teams have also developed moves using the hookers as the extra player, staying wide of the ruck or maul to create an overlap. The hooker should have good leg speed and be a good tackler on the short side of the lineout (the gap between lineout and touchline).

> **Main skills: Hooking the ball back in the scrum; throwing the ball into the lineout**
> **Main practice: Scrummaging and throwing the ball into the lineout**

Lock

The two tallest people in the team almost always become the locks (or second row forwards), whose job it is to win the ball at the lineouts. They are also required to lend their weight in the scrums. Locks should be strong and rugged; along with the front row they are the tight forwards (the tight five), who are expected to do the hard work at the rucks, mauls and scrums. In the modern game, locks are also expected to be mobile.

> **Main skills: Catching lineout ball; scrummaging**
> **Main practice: Jumping for and catching lineout ball; scrummaging**

No. 8

The No. 8 is a key man at scrum time because he is able to link with the backs. He is the only forward allowed to pick up the ball from the back of the scrum. He should have a good, almost telepathic, understanding with the scrum-half.

Below: Dan van Zyl discovers that lock forwards, such as the Wellington Hurricanes' Dion Waller, can tackle.

Right: The prime role of a lock is to catch the ball in the lineout — Northern Bulls' Kraynouw Otto at full stretch.

The ideal No. 8 should be a mix of all the forwards: big and tough, but also intelligent and skilful. He must also be mobile and a good tackler.

Main skills: Tackling; running with the ball in hand
Main practice: Tackling; linking with scrum-half

Below: A No. 8 must be big and strong to take the ball up. Australia's Tiaan Strauss charges into the Welsh defence.

Right: A flanker's main role is to tackle. Wales' No. 7 Colin Charvis closes down Argentina's Diego Albanese.

Flanker

The flankers are the loose forwards who stand on the sides or 'flanks' of the scrum. A flanker's job is to get to the ball as quickly as possible. Some teams play with a right and left flanker who always stay on their own sides of the scrum, but these days most teams play with an open-side and a blind-side flanker.

The scrum is set at the exact position where play breaks down. Usually there is a larger distance to the touchline on one side of the scrum than the other. The side with the greatest distance is called the **open side** and the side with the shortest distance is called the **blind side**.

The **open-side flanker** should be the fittest player in the team. His task is to be the first player to the ball when play breaks down. An open-side flanker should also have the explosive speed of a back. At training he should practice with the backs often, to improve his speed and his ball-handling skills.

The **blind-side flanker** is more of a cross between a lock and an open-side flanker. He should also be fit and fast, as well as tall and strong. His additional size and strength is required for blind-side defence and his height for options at the back of the lineout. Both flankers must be excellent tacklers.

Main skills: Tackling; reading the play; fitness
Main practice: Tackling; running

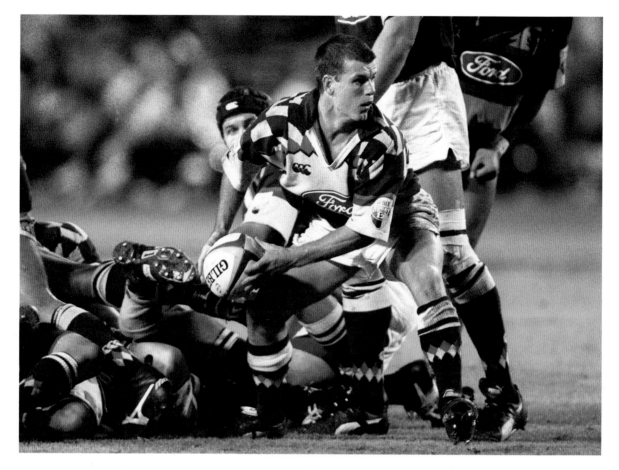

Scrum-half

The scrum-half is often the smallest player in the team as he has to bend low to retrieve the ball from the back of the scrum or ruck. He is the link between backs and forwards. Passing is the key skill of the scrum-half. His pass must be fast, long and accurate and he should be able to do it equally well off either hand.

The scrum-half must be a quick thinker, frequently having to decide whether to leave the ball with the forwards, pass to the backs, go left or right, kick, or run with it himself. He would usually run with the ball at least twice during a game to keep the opposition guessing. The best scrum-halves have a fast turn of speed from a standing start, especially over 10–25 metres.

The scrum-half should also have the confidence to tell his forwards when and how he wants the ball.

> Main skills: Passing, decision-making
> Main practice: Long passing off either hand

Above: The scrum-half is the link between the forwards and the backs. Auckland Blues' scrum-half Steve Devine fires the ball out.

Fly-half

The fly-half should possess a range of skills with the ball in hand and off the foot. He should be particularly good at punting the ball long distances upfield or into touch to relieve opposition pressure. He is often an elusive runner, good at sidesteps and deception, and able to set up opportunities for the faster runners outside him.

He should also be tactically aware: his place on the field — and the protection he gets from opposition tacklers by the long pass of his scrum-half — is the best to get a clear view of the options available. A fly-half must be a good tackler as in modern rugby opposition players often target this position. He also plays a covering role, running behind his backs to cut off opposition attacks.

Main skills: Kicking
Main practice: Kicking, especially punting

Right: One of the main duties of a fly-half is to make long punts down field. All Black Andrew Mehrtens clears.

Centre

There are two centres. They can play as left and right centre, or as inside and outside centre (the inside is always closer to the scrum).

Centres must be fast runners, good tacklers and excellent passers, especially good at timing a pass to their fleet-footed wings. The inside centre should be skilled at creating doubt in the minds of the opposition — to have them guessing which way the play is going. In the modern game he is also used as a battering ram to set up second phase possession.

Main skills: Tackling; passing
Main practice: Tackling; timing the pass

Below: A centre's role, as shown by Manu Samoa's Va'aiga Tuigamala, is to get behind the line and set up his wing, in this case Brian Lima at right.

Right: Christian Cullen, here playing at centre, uses a side-step to beat the Tongan defence.

Wing

The wings should be the fastest players in the team. They should be able to create the space in which to run and should have the ability to score tries. (The leading tryscorers in international rugby are wings.) There was a time when many wings were small and elusive, relying on deception and sheer speed; nowadays wings are generally bigger and stronger to counter the improved defensive strategies of modern rugby.

Main skills: Speed; ability to beat a man
Main practice: Sprint training

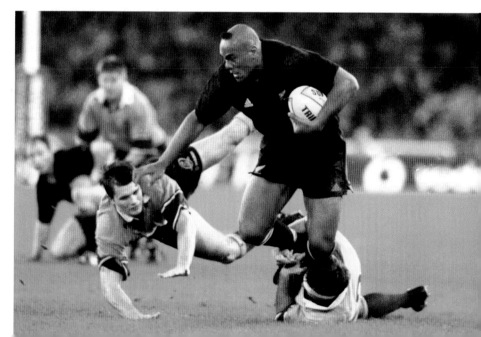

Right: A winger usually tries to get past his opposite on the outside. A desperate Australian defence just foils Jonah Lomu on this occasion.

Fullback

A fullback should be able to tackle like a centre, have the speed of a wing and possess the kicking skills of a fly-half. He should be very good at catching the high ball, especially under pressure.

In the early days of rugby the role of the fullback was almost completely defensive. Today the fullback is a key attacking weapon, entering the backline to create an 'extra man' for his team.

Main skills: Catching the high ball; tackling, defensive cover, timing his entry into the line
Main practice: Catching the high ball and kicking it, either upfield or into touch

Right: A fullback's main role is to take the high ball. Jeff Wilson has over run the ball slightly, but still manages to catch it securely.

In the 1950s the great All Black fullback George Nepia was still taking part in charity matches. In one of them he scored a unique try. The ball came straight to him after a clearance, he saw a gap in the defence, and went straight through to score under the post. What made it unique was that he was the referee at the time!

Below: By coming into the line, fullback Shane Howarth, here playing for Wales, adds an extra man and changes the angle of attack.

2

The Basic Skills: Running

There are five basic skills of rugby that *every* player should possess. They are running, passing, catching, tackling and attitude. These are the foundations of all team play. A planned move fails only when a basic skill fails (such as dropping the ball). And running is the most basic of all rugby skills.

Run straight

Unless attempting to evade an individual tackler, players should generally run straight ahead. Imagine the rugby field to be made up of lanes; don't run in someone else's lane, otherwise the attack will drift sideways and run out of space near the sidelines.

Run towards support

The ball carrier should always be aware of his support players. When going forward, he should try to make it easy for his support to get to him.

Running after the ball

The general rule in defence is that forwards run after the ball, while the backs maintain their defensive positions. Players should also learn to 'read' the play so that they can arrive at a point on the field at the same time as the ball.

Support play

Support players should always position themselves where they can receive a pass. When there are several players in support they should spread out on either side of the ball carrier so that the

Rugby is a running game. South Africa's Robbie Fleck in full flight in the 1999 World Cup semifinal against Australia.

attack resembles an arrowhead formation. Support players should follow a forward more closely to take a short pass or to join the ruck or maul that may form.

Support play wins matches. Players should be fit enough to keep up with the play. An attack only really breaks down when it runs out of support.

Carrying the ball

The ball can be carried in one or both hands. A player can run faster with the ball in one hand, but he has more options available and a better chance of deceiving his opponents when he runs with the ball in two hands. Generally a player should only hold the ball in one hand if he is free of the opposition, fending off an opposing player or charging forward.

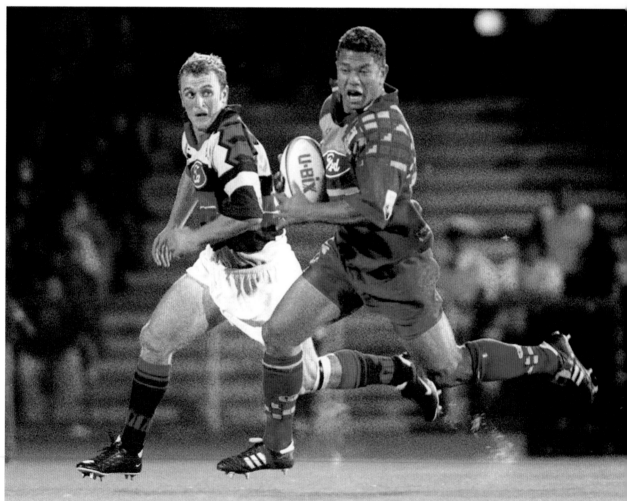

Above left: Superb ball carrying technique from Breyton Paulse. He is perfectly balanced and holds the ball in two hands. He is set to sprint, evade or pass.

Above: Scotland's Shaun Longstaff is drifting right, in the direction of his support player Chris Paterson.

Above right: France's Emile Ntamack is also heading in the direction of his support players, which will enable him to keep the ball alive if the Argentinian defenders are able to stop him.

Left: Aggression, pace and balance — Otago Highlanders' Pita Alatini shows the qualities needed when making a break.

Right: Pieter Rossouw has been tackled but his hands are free and he is looking for a support player.

When holding the ball in one hand, the ball is tucked tight against the chest, though some players do have big enough hands to grasp it quite securely with only one hand. The ball should always be held in the hand farthest away from the nearest opponent. If a closer opponent approaches from the other side, the ball should be transferred to the other hand.

Above: Christian Cullen has swerved around one opponent and prepares to fend off another. Note his perfectly balanced running style.

The forward charge

The player charging forward runs at full speed straight at an opponent. The ball is held firmly in one or two hands and hugged tightly against the chest or stomach so that it won't be knocked

Right: The forward charge as exemplified by Welsh prop Garin Jenkins — low body position, bristling aggression, ball secure and Craig Quinell in support.

34

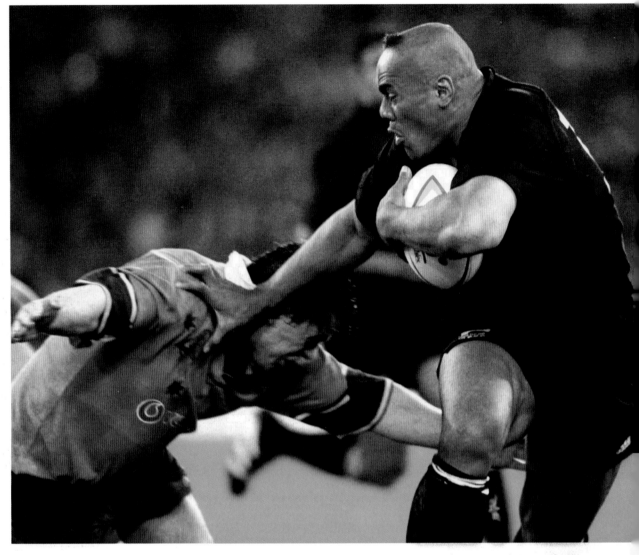

loose at the moment of impact. When the player is two or three paces away from the tackler, he lowers his shoulder and aims it at the tackler, trying to knock him over or out of the way. If he beats the tackler, he continues on to the next tackler.

The fend or hand-off

The attacker runs straight at the defender, the ball safely tucked up in his furthermost arm. As he gets within touching distance, he reaches out with the nearest arm, which is bent, and straightens it immediately at the moment of contact, pushing the tackler away and at the same time pushing himself off the tackler. He then has to accelerate away before the tackler recovers.

Above: Jonah Lomu fending off Wallaby Rod Kafer. The arm is straight at the point of contact but he is already starting to accelerate away.

Top right: England's Lawrence Dallaglio has managed to spin out of this hit by the Italian defender.

Right: Chris Wyatt of Wales is unsuccessful with this bump because Argentina's Octavio Bartolucci has managed to get his arms around him.

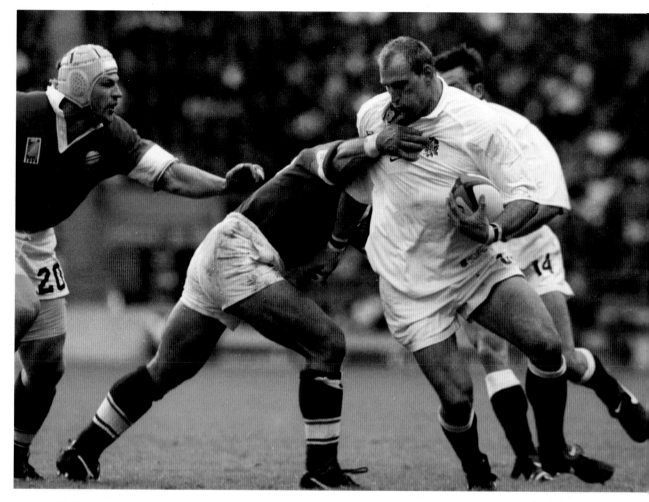

The hit and spin

This is a forward charge in which the attacking player, instead of making full impact with the tackler, spins out of the impact and keeps running (or he spins round to pass the ball to a team-mate). The attacker's shoulder is dropped into the lower body of the defender. He then drives on the side where his body overlaps that of the defender, twisting his hips, taking small steps and spinning out of the tackle.

The bump

The bump is a version of the forward charge and is especially useful if the tackler has set himself low. As the attacker comes into the tackle he suddenly lowers his body and gives the tackler a shove with his shoulder. This cannot be done if the tackler is set high for the tackle.

Deceptive running

The ball carrier will often use deception and balance to beat a tackler. Deception relies on making the tackler think twice, causing him to hesitate. Balance relies on the ball carrier sensing which foot the tackler's weight is mostly on, and going that way. There are several versions of deceptive running.

The swerve

The attacker runs straight at the tackler, but about three or so paces away, he starts to curve his run away from the tackler, still running fast, and passes him beyond his reach.

Above: An outside swerve by Christian Cullen leaves an English defender sprawled on the ground behind him.

Right: Kees Meeuws, a very mobile prop, darts through a gap in the South African defence.

Above: Damian Karauna of the Wellington Hurricanes thrusts off his right leg to side-step to the left.

Outside cut (also known as an 'in and out')

Like a swerve, except the lines taken are straighter and is only done near the touchline. The attacker runs towards the defender, then makes as if to cut inside him. As the defender stops or hesitates, the attacker changes the angle sharply to the outside and sprints away (Jonah Lomu's favourite move).

The side-step

The attacking player gets as close as he can to the tackler without the tackler being able to reach him, then slows suddenly by taking a short step. He drops his shoulder in the direction he is going to step, thrusting with the opposite leg, effectively moving sideways at speed. As soon as he has stepped to the side of the tackler, he must straighten up and accelerate to get clear of him.

Dodge or dart

A very sudden change of direction to left or right, angled away from the tackler. Like the feint (see opposite), the shoulder leans toward the defender before short, rapid steps take the attacking player beyond his reach.

Above: The skill of running includes the ability to slip the tackle, which Jonah Lomu manages to do here by maintaining his speed and intensity.

Left: By carrying the ball in two hands the USA's Kevin Dalzell has all options open and the Romanian defence seems uncertain.

The prop

A version of the side-step in which only a small step is taken, immediately followed by a hard push off one leg to get past the tackler.

The feint

The attacker drops a shoulder implying that he is going one way, but does not, so deceiving the tackler.

The goose step

Two or three quick steps where the legs are lifted up with the knee locked. It suggests to the defender that a change of pace or direction is about to occur, causing him to hesitate. Instead, the player takes off at speed. Used to great effect by the great Australian wing, David Campese.

The full stop

The full stop is when the attacker comes to a sudden stop, confusing the defenders, who are likely to stop also. Then the attacker takes off again, gaining three or four vital metres in the process.

> When the Fijians went to Britain in 1970, one or two jokers in the squad enjoyed playing up their 'primitive' background. A young agency reporter on one of his first assignments made the mistake of asking a large Fijian forward how they celebrated after their matches. 'The winners eat the losers,' he replied.

Right: Even better than slipping a tackle is avoiding it altogether; Jonah's pace doesn't allow his opponent to get within reach.

3

The Basic Skills: Passing

Passing is the main skill that makes rugby a team game. One of the fundamental rules of the game is that the ball cannot be passed forward. It can only be passed in a line level with the receiver or, more usually, behind that line.

The theory is that you pass the ball to a team-mate who is in a better position than you. If he and the rest of the team are then able to continue to pass the ball to a team-mate who is always in a better position, sooner or later, one of the players will be in the best position of all — the position to score a try.

Normal pass

The whole body is used to pass the ball. It is coiled like a spring to add greater velocity, distance and accuracy to the pass.

The player runs forward with the ball in two hands. He swings the ball across his body in the opposite direction to which he is going to pass it. His weight will be on the opposite leg. His shoulders will be twisted slightly away from the direction in which he is going to pass.

Then his arms and shoulders swing back in the direction of the pass with a slight sway of the hips. The legs cross and the body as a whole falls away from the direction of the pass as the ball is propelled.

When to pass

The ball carrier should pass the ball to another player on his own side who is in a better position to maintain the attack than himself. This is usually when the ball carrier is about to be tackled or

When to pass? Christian Cullen will be aware that Craig Dowd is in support to his left. Dowd is already looking ahead to put himself in a position to receive the ball if Cullen chooses to pass to him.

his way forward is obstructed. A pass also changes the point of attack which means the defending team has to reset. If the ball can be passed faster than the defending team can reset, a try is often the result.

The ball carrier should not pass the ball to a player in a position where he is likely to be tackled as soon as he gets the ball. This bad pass is known as a 'hospital pass' because that is where the receiver could end up!

Aiming the pass

A pass should be made *to* a team-mate, not just flung in his general direction. The ball should arrive at the receiver between waist and chest in a way, and at a speed, that it can be easily caught. If the receiver is running, the ball must be thrown in front of him so that he can run onto it and catch it without breaking stride. It is the responsibility of the passer to make it as easy as possible for the receiver to catch the ball.

Left: Good passing technique from Tony Brown. The arms have swung across his body, his leg has crossed, his whole body is ready to launch the ball to his right.

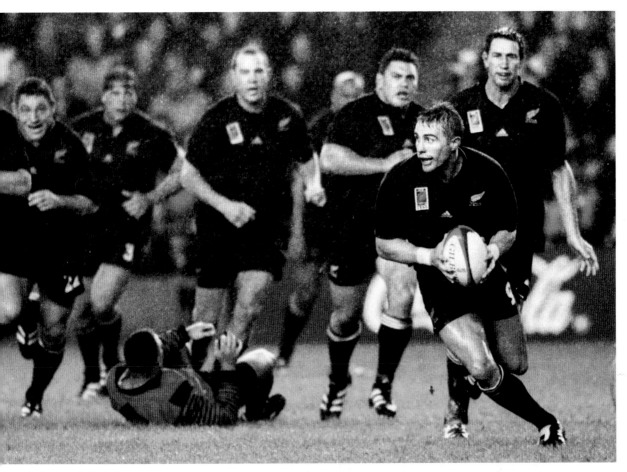

Above: Justin Marshall has many passing options open to him as his support players come through. Note Taine Randell (extreme left), who is making it clear to Marshall that he is ready to receive the ball.

Passing: the ball travels quicker than the man.

Timing the pass

Timing the pass is very important. Perfect timing can create sufficient space for an attacking team to gain an advantage that might result in a try. The passer might pass early to allow the receiver more space in which to run or he might pass late after committing a defender. Timing is a matter of judgement in each situation.

Passing on

Passing on is the term used to shift the ball out wide. The player receiving the ball passes it as soon as he has received it.

Drawing the man

When the ball carrier is marked by a defender and the player he is going to pass to is unmarked, the ball carrier delays his pass until the last possible moment. If he were to pass the ball straight away the defender would have time to tackle the new ball carrier. So

45

the ball carrier draws (attracts) the defender by running straight at him as if he were going to evade him. Just before the defender makes the tackle, the ball carrier passes the ball to his team-mate, too late for the defender to tackle the receiver.

Delaying the pass

Sometimes an advantage is gained by holding onto the ball a little longer, either to fool the defence or to allow time for a team-mate to come through at speed. The delayed pass gives the receiving player the space and time to break the line. This is a great skill which almost always produces results for the attacking team.

Different types of passes

Spin or spiral pass

In this pass, the hand opposite the direction of the pass comes up over the ball as the pass is thrown, causing the ball to spin. A spinning ball travels quicker than a non-spinning ball — due to less air resistance — which in turn means the trajectory of the ball can be flatter and less likely to be intercepted.

Below: Kevin Dalzell of the USA fires out a spin pass to his fly-half (extreme right of picture) who will take it on the run.

Scrum-half pass

This is a specialist pass by the scrum-half to clear the ball from the forwards out to the backs. It must be done quickly, before the opposition defence pours through, and in a single movement from first touch of the ball to its release.

While awaiting delivery of the ball, the scrum-half must set himself 'cocked like a gun' ready to fire the ball immediately. He does not glance at the receiver while waiting for the ball because this alerts the defenders that the ball is coming out.

If he is passing left, his right foot is nearest the ball. The other foot is positioned about a hip's width away pointing towards the receiver. The knees are slightly bent.

The arms are extended so that as soon as he receives the ball, he swings his arms through a wide arc, with the force of his whole body. It is vital that the pass is made all in one motion. Precious time is lost if the scrum-half has to wind up for the swing or take any steps. Most scrum-halves also make the ball spin for greater speed and distance.

> Thomas Gordon's misfortune was to lose his right hand in a shooting accident at an early age. Nonetheless, he played three times for Ireland in the 1870s as a three-quarter, and is thought to be the only one-handed player to appear in international rugby.

Right: Justin Marshall with perfect body position, fully unwound as he unleashes a long pass from the base of the scrum.

Long pass

Any pass which is thrown a long distance.

American football pass

Some players have adopted the American football style of pass for throwing long. The ball is held in one hand, pulled back over the shoulder and hurled like a spinning javelin. Of course in rugby, unlike American football, this pass cannot be thrown forward.

Dive pass

This is a quick pass used by the scrum-half when he has not been able to get himself into the proper position for a long pass. The ball is gripped in both hands and thrown from below the waist through the length of his body in a scooping motion as he dives forward, releasing it when his arms are at full stretch. This is a very effective way of clearing the ball quickly when the scrum-half is under pressure from the opposition.

Reverse pass

The reverse pass is a variation of the long pass in which the scrum-half has his back to the receiver. He throws the ball out of the back of his hand and behind his back, with the hand coming over the ball to create spin. As the scrum-half is virtually throwing blind, he has to be aware of the position of the receiver.

Above: Pieter Rossouw acts as a scrum-half at a ruck. Because of the fast flowing nature of rucks, any player must be prepared to take on the role of scrum-half.

Above left: Perfect technique from Byron Kelleher. Speed is of the essence before the Sharks' scrum-half Hentie Martens can get to him.

Right: The full, spectacular extension of the dive pass by Manu Samoa's Steven So'oialo.

Lob pass

The lob pass is a deliberate, high-looping toss of the ball which takes it over the heads of defenders to a team-mate. It may have spin on it.

Pop pass

The pop pass is a very short pass: the ball is simply 'popped up' in a small loop to a player who is coming through at speed.

Below: Joost Van Der Westhuizen winds up for a dive pass.

Unusual passes

There are a variety of passes that can be used in special situations. In many of these cases, the ball is passed using only the arms and hands — without the force and weight of the body — and sometimes just the hands.

Above: Matt Dawson is tackled and falling, but he still has enough control of the ball to slip a one-handed pass to his support.

Flick pass

The flick pass is a short pass thrown quickly with a flick of the wrists.

Fast pass

The fast pass is when the player receiving the ball is about to be tackled. He treats the ball like a hot potato: the moment it touches his hands, he flicks it straight on to a team-mate.

Tackled ball pass

The tackled ball pass is any type of pass the tackled player can use to free the ball to a team-mate.

One-handed pass

The one-handed pass can be used when a tackled or falling player is able to unload the ball with only one hand.

Right: Byron Kelleher flips the ball out of the back of his hand, though on this occasion it looks like he has had a quick look first.

Overhead pass

The overhead pass is lobbing the ball with one hand over a defender's head to pass to a team-mate.

Change-of-direction pass

The change-of-direction pass is intended to deceive: when it seems the ball carrier is about to pass the ball one way, he holds onto it, twists around, and passes it another way.

All passing should be practised to the left and to the right.

The reverse flick

A player running forward knows — or gets a call — that a team-mate is following behind. Without looking he flicks the ball back to him out of the back of his hand. When successful this pass can be devastating because no one expects it and it can easily change the direction of the attack.

The 'anything goes' pass

The whole point of passing is to get the ball into the hands of a team-mate who is in a better position. In a tackled ball situation or crowded traffic, a player might invent all sorts of ways of passing the ball. If he gets it into the hands of a team-mate who is in a better position than himself, no matter how untidy or unorthodox the pass might appear, it is a good pass.

Below: It's not pretty, but Craig Dowd has made the 'perfect pass' because he has managed to free the ball to his support player Tana Umaga.

Above: Going backwards in the pouring rain, Colin Charvis has fallen on the loose ball to prevent Australians Tim Horan (left) and Daniel Herbert from getting it.

In wet weather the ball can be very slippery. Players should stand about a metre closer together and passes should be shorter and easier to take. In hot weather, when the ball and hands are dry, passes can be crisper and faster.

Deceptive passes

There are many ways of deceiving members of the opposing team when it come to passing, or not passing, the ball. When executed well, they can be very effective.

The dummy pass

The ball carrier goes through all the preliminary motions of passing the ball, but at the moment of release he holds onto it and darts through a gap. The trick with this is that if the ball carrier himself *believes* he is going to pass the ball, so will the defenders. Similarly, the ball carrier might appear as if he is about to kick: when the tackler hesitates, he makes for a gap, ball in hand.

The non-pass

A version of the dummy pass: the ball carrier is running at speed with the ball in one hand. He then clasps it with both hands, slows slightly as if about to pass, and suddenly takes off again.

Decoy

Not so much a pass as a runner who pretends he is about to take a pass. Decoys are very useful at set-piece situations — defenders are unsure what direction the attack is going to come from.

4

The Basic Skills: Catching

When a ball is passed to a player, no matter how bad the pass might be, it is his job to catch it. When he fails to do so and the ball is lost forward it is called a 'knock-on'. If the opposing side gains an advantage because of the knock-on, the referee may allow play to continue, but if there's no advantage, the referee will stop play and award a scrum with the put-in given to the opposing side. There is no excuse for dropping the ball. Catching is a skill and like any other skill it can be perfected with practice.

Catching a pass

Even before the pass is made, the catcher should position himself to receive it. He lets the ball carrier know he is there and is expecting the ball. This can be done through eye contact, shouting or even his body language showing he is prepared to receive the ball. Similarly, the catcher should be able to read the body language of the passer so that he knows when to expect the pass.

The catcher should be to one side of the ball carrier, about 3–5 metres away (closer if the ball carrier is a forward on the charge). He should be coming up from a deeper position and running at maximum speed, timing his run so that he receives the ball when almost level with the passer. He should also angle his run to put himself in a better attacking position than the player who passed the ball.

The catcher should keep his eye on the ball until it is firmly in his hands. Though he might be tempted to plan what he is going to do with the ball, thinking too far ahead or worrying about the opposition tackler has caused many a knock-on. The ball should

The Auckland Blues on attack: Carlos Spencer gets the pass away with Joeli Vindiri in good position to accept it.

Left: Good technique by the USA's Mark Williams as he takes the high ball. He looks like he has called for a mark, but he should get a penalty because the tackler has grabbed him in the air — illegally.

Below: Bruce Reihana has climbed high because of the presence of Canterbury Crusaders players, but he has not kept his eye on the ball and spilled it.

be caught in both hands, fingers splayed outwards to fasten onto the ball, which is then clasped to the chest.

Catching bad passes

A bad pass could end up behind the catcher, over his head or around his toes. The catcher should decide if the ball is within reach. If it isn't he should leave it, so avoiding a possible knock-on.

If the ball is catchable, no matter how bad the pass, it his job to catch it. To achieve this, he should practice catching bad passes, not only standing still, but on the run.

Catching from a kick

When catching a high ball from a kick the catcher must keep his eyes on the ball and judge precisely where it will land. He must call loudly, indicating to his team-mates nearby that he intends to catch it, thus avoiding a possible collision. Once he has positioned himself underneath the ball, he splays his fingers and cups his arms to make a 'basket' against his chest into which the ball will fall. Then he immediately tightens his grip around it. The key is to keep your eyes on the ball until it is safely caught.

If a player thinks an opponent might beat him to the ball, he should be prepared to jump for it, either straight up from a stationary start or after a run of several paces, thus gaining the momentum to leap even higher.

Catching the ball behind his own 22-metre line allows a player to claim a mark (fair catch) by shouting 'mark'. If the referee awards it the player is given a free kick. However, do not wait for the referee's whistle — he might not consider it a fair catch or he may have been unsighted — but immediately continue on with the game.

Catching basics: Keep your eye on the ball, concentrate, and spread your fingers and arms in such a way that you maximise your chances of catching it securely. Catching is a skill that can be perfected with practice.

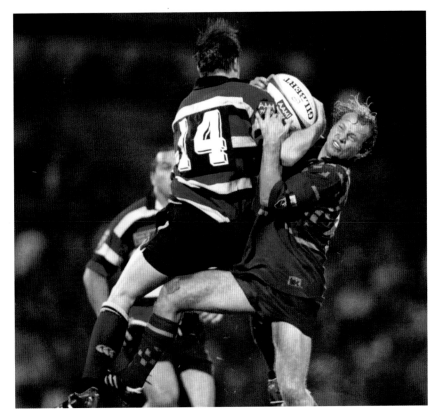

Right: Ben Tune and Tony Brown competing for the high ball. Concentration and timing are the key.

No opposition player is allowed to *tackle* the catcher in the air, though he can be challenged for the ball.

At kick restarts, when opposition players are jumping against them, forwards should be able to catch the ball cleanly above their heads.

Catching near the touchline

When a player is attempting to catch the ball near the touchline he should be aware of his proximity to the line. When a penalty kick is aimed at the touchline, the player receiving the ball should stand two or three paces off the field so that he is able to run forward to catch a weak kick landing in the field of play. Even while off the field, as long as the ball does not cross the line, he is allowed to bat the ball back into the field of play with his hands — but it must go backwards.

Picking up a bobbing ball

When the ball has been kicked along the ground the receiver must be careful to judge the uneven bounce so that he does not knock it on when attempting to control it. If in any doubt, he should stop the ball with his foot and then pick it up.

Picking up the ball off the ground

Players should also practise picking up a stationary ball off the ground at speed, by running forward and scooping it up with one or both hands.

Falling on the ball

Falling on the ball is a great skill. It is usually done when the ball has gone loose behind the defensive line and opponents are coming through. The defending player runs back towards his own line, falls on the ball and gathers it up in such a way that he is able to regain his feet immediately.

Right: Christian Cullen and Tana Umaga both compete for the high ball because of the presence of a French player. If there was no opposition, one of them, the nearest player, should call for the ball.

Catching a wet ball is much harder than catching a dry ball. Practise by soaking a rugby ball in water and wetting your hands. Use washing-up liquid to make the ball even more slippery.

Below: Christian Cullen displays good catching technique. Eyes on the ball, arms spread and fingers splayed ready to catch it.

Bad weather has spoilt many a sporting fixture, and on many occasions rugby grounds have been turned into unplayable boggy snowfields. One of the coldest venues must be Russia. On 19 October 1978, when Poly Technika Alma Ata played Krasnoyarsk, the temperature was recorded at minus 23°C. All the players wore gloves, tracksuits and balaclavas in an attempt to shield themselves from the Siberian blast. The game couldn't be cancelled as the visitors had travelled approximately 2000 km to get there.

5

The Basic Skills: Tackling

Tackling is as basic to rugby as running. Full bodily contact is allowed but without any form of striking.

Four elements comprise a **tackle** — courage, judgement, technique and timing. If a young player is unsure about tackling, he should practise the different parts of the tackle as laid out in this book until he can do them all in one fluid motion. With correct technique, the smallest player can tackle the largest. Tackling is not a difficult skill to master and it is a very satisfying feeling to execute the perfect tackle and dump your opponent on the turf.

The original meaning of the word tackle is to grab hold of the ropes that control the sails of a sailing ship. In rugby the idea is the same — to grab hold of your opponent in order to control or restrict his progress. This can be achieved by putting him on the ground, lifting him off the ground or by turning him around to face *your* team.

Tackling is very important to defensive patterns. General defensive pressure can also result in obtaining possession of the ball by forcing the opposition to make mistakes.

A normal front-on tackle

The four main elements of a tackle are courage, judgement, technique and timing. This is how these four elements translate when making a normal front-on tackle:

Courage

Courage comes from certainty. The tackler lines up the ball carrier and prepares for the tackle by making a rapid judgement of

The perfect head-on tackle by Afato So'oalo: a low body position and driving hard into the middle of the body. A pained look from Joeli Vidiri completes the picture.

61

Left: Scotland's Gordon Bulloch lines up Andrew Mehrtens for a low front-on tackle.

Right: David Edwards of Tonga has a hand on Tana Umaga but needs to get more of a grip to prevent him from bursting out of the tackle.

distance, speed and direction. He does not look at the player's eyes or at his hands because he could be deceived by his body language. He looks at the player's legs to judge which way he might try to step or swerve, and focuses on the tackle.

The four main elements of a tackle are courage, judgement, technique and timing.

Judgement

Focusing on the tackle means deciding which tackle he will make. He could try to knock the player back or over the touchline; he might use a smother tackle, try to turn him, or hold him up and steal the ball.

The calculations include where on the tackler's body he will make the hit. He is allowed to make the tackle anywhere between the knees and the chest. All this will go through his mind in a second or two. With practice and experience he will reach the stage where he will instinctively make the right choice in each situation.

A key part of the tackle is closing the gap. The tackler must choose the line of approach along which he is most likely to intercept the ball carrier and make the hit.

Technique

Having made the decisions the tackler must now block everything else from his mind and concentrate on the tackle. He should be totally fearless. He should lean towards the ball carrier, back

Right: A spectacular side-on tackle by the New South Wales Waratahs' Scott Staniforth wraps up Jeff Wilson.

straight, aiming with the nearest shoulder. The main thrust will come from the legs, which should be bent just before impact.

The tackler's head is to the side of the ball carrier's body. His shoulder impacts against the target zone and drives the ball carrier's body backwards and upwards.

The tackler's arms 'embrace' the ball carrier at waist level, dropping down behind his thighs, and pulling them forwards.

The ball carrier becomes the victim of opposing forces: one force (the tackler's shoulder) is pushing his upper body back, the other force (behind the thighs) is pulling his lower body forward. He is effectively being cut in half and knocked off balance.

At this point, the tackler puts all his weight into the impact, forcing the ball carrier backwards, smashing him into the ground and landing on top of him.

Right: This tackle shows good technique, but the Australian is too late. Pieter Rossouw will slip the ball to his support players.

Timing

The critical component of any tackle is timing. The most effective hit is when the ball carrier is at his most vulnerable — in mid-stride perhaps, or when he is slightly unbalanced in the process of trying to side-step. Timing can only really be learned by practising tackling against team-mates (suitably padded). When teams practice only on tackle bags, they are only really practising one part of the tackle — the hit.

Even when the hit has been made, the tackle is not over. The reason for the tackle is to dispossess the ball carrier. The tackler must quickly get to his feet and make every attempt to secure the ball.

Tackling variations

Left: Richard Dourthe of France has been able to obstruct Jonah Lomu, but he has been unable to complete the tackle.

There are several ways of tackling the ball carrier that can be equally effective if they present the defending team with an opportunity to win the ball.

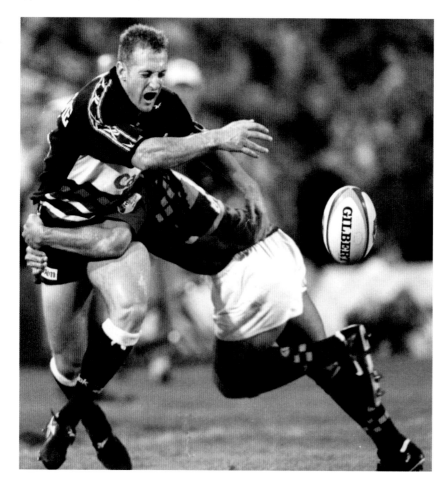

Above: Even with two of them, these French players don't look very happy about tackling Jonah Lomu.

Left: A crunching side-on tackle by Brian Lima forces Stefan Terblanche to spill the ball.

The half hold

Sometimes, in a match situation, the tackler is unable to complete the tackle, in which case he should at least hold on to the ball carrier and impede his progress until he, or one of his own team-mates, can finish off the tackle.

Side-on tackle

In the side-on tackle, the shoulder is thrust into the ball carrier's waist just above the hips. The arms go around the waist/hips area then slide down the attacker's thighs while still maintaining a firm hold. As the hold tightens, the ball carrier's legs will be pulled tighter together and his momentum will take him to the ground.

Tackle from behind

This is similar to the side-on tackle except the tackler pursues the ball carrier and takes him from behind. The tackler aims for the

Above: Christian Cullen has run down France's Christophe Dominici and catches him with a diving tackle from behind.

Left: A Wellington Hurricanes' player has made the hit from the side and is starting to wrap his arms around Daryl Gibson, ready to drag him to the ground.

target area — the small of the back down to just below the buttocks — and envelops the waist or hips with his arms, sliding down the ball carrier's legs and bringing his run to an abrupt end.

The ankle tap

If unable to get close enough from behind to make the tackle, the tackler can strike the ankles of the ball carrier. He dives forward and knocks the nearest ankle of the ball carrier against the other, causing him to trip. The defender must then get to his feet before the ball carrier and make an effort to complete the tackle or dispossess him.

Stationary tackle

If the tackler is stationary and the ball carrier is moving towards him at speed, the tackler should just 'accept' the tackle. The ball carrier will try to 'run through' the would-be tackler, so the tackler should brace himself for the impact, get a firm hold and allow the ball carrier's momentum to take them both to the ground.

The big hit

One of the best tackles, which often happens in the centres, is when a player from the defending team is able to read an opposition pass and arrives just as an attacking player receives the ball. The attacker will have his eye on the ball, so the defender can smash him backwards at the instant he receives the pass. This 'big hit' always looks spectacular.

Smother tackle

In the smother tackle the defender's target is higher on the ball carrier's body, usually around the chest. There is less shoulder used and more emphasis on wrapping the arms around those of the attacker so that he is unable to pass the ball to a team-mate.

Right: Franco Smith has his head to the side of Pita Alatini's body, his back is straight, his body position low and his arms gripping behind Alatini's legs. Alatini's face shows that he knows he has lost control of the situation.

Below: Afato So'oalo again: this time his aim is a little higher and his right arm smothers the ball, making it very difficult for his opponent to release it to his support.

Driving tackle

The attacker is upright and in a poor driving position, while the defender is leaning forward in a low driving position and pumping his legs hard. In this way the ball carrier can often be driven backwards several metres, gaining an advantage for the defending team.

Touchline tackling

When tackling close to the touchline, the defending team should always try to drive the ball carrier over the touchline to gain the throw-in to the lineout. Prior to the tackle being made, the tackler should position himself so as to force the ball carrier closer to the touchline. At the moment of impact, he completes the tackle with a rapid leg drive and a low body position. Alternatively, the tackled player can be pushed or dragged over the touchline.

Below: Lisandro Arbizu of Argentina has forced Gareth Thomas of Wales close to the touchline and tackled him out of play.

Left: The Australian player has gone lower for this tackle against South Africa's Jannie de Beer. The hold will tighten around the knees, dragging him to the ground.

Turning the player in the tackle

In this tackle, the ball carrier is turned towards the opposing team's forwards. If the ball carrier has already been stopped and is upright, one or more of the defending team should grab hold of him and turn him their way.

It is much more difficult to turn a player in the tackle itself, a hallmark of a very skilled tackler. The tackler sets for a normal tackle but instead of trying to knock the ball carrier back, he allows him to come through and slips behind him. He then holds him so that his team-mates can rip the ball from him.

Tackling a bigger player

Any player can tackle any other player on a rugby field no matter what their size. But a very small player would not normally expect to knock back a much bigger player in the tackle. The better option would be to use a technique similar to the stationary tackle. With courage and timing he can use the attacker's own weight and momentum to take him to ground, as in judo.

Right: Italy's Massimo Giovanelli uses his weight to bring down England's Phil Vickery.

Below: The minimum requirement of a tackle is to get a hold on the player, but Jonah Lomu has skipped (or slipped) out of this attempt by Tonga's Elisi Vunipola.

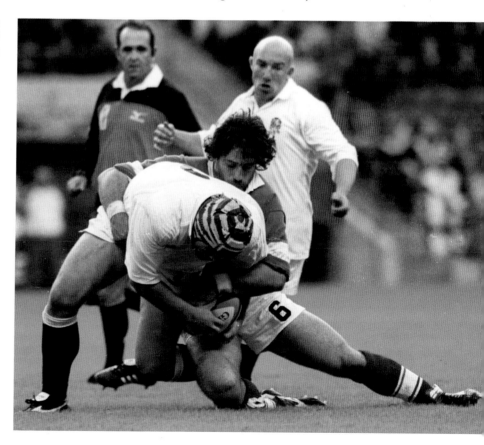

Above: Reuben Thorne has gone high on Tonga's Semi Taupeaafe and looks like he is getting a piggy back, but his body weight will slow Taupeaafe down.

Above left: Argentina's Ignacio Fernandez seems to have executed the tackle, except Manu Samoa's Pat Lam still has control of the ball and seems set to pass.

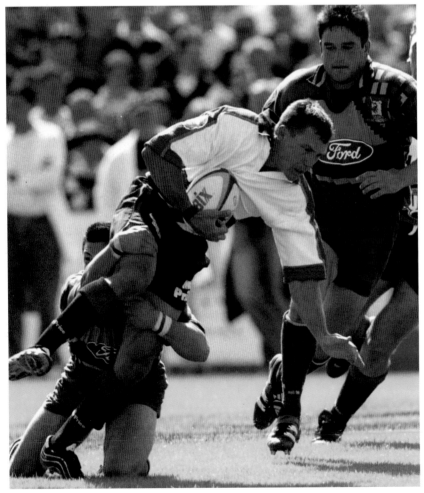

Left: Byron Kelleher has gone low on Andre Snyman, tying up his legs, causing him to lose his balance and fall to the ground.

Gang tackling

Two or more players can tackle the ball carrier at the same time, especially when the ball carrier is bigger than usual.

Tackling the fend

When the ball carrier tries to fend off the tackler, the tackler has two options. He can go below the arm and use a powerful leg drive to break through the fend, or he can grab the fending arm and use it as a half hold to get in closer and make a proper tackle.

The perfect tackle

A tackler should always try to execute the perfect tackle, and for his own protection he should always use the proper technique. However, it must be remembered that the reason for the tackle is to get in the way of the ball carrier, get a hold of him, slow him down and give the tackler's team a chance to get the ball. If he manages to do all of these things, he has executed the perfect tackle.

Right: Auckland Blues' Craig Innes has made the hit on the Golden Cats' Thinus Delport and looks set to complete the tackle.

Below: Doug Howlett has nowhere to go in this twin tackle by Corne Krige and Breyton Paulse of the Western Stormers.

6

The Basic Skills: Attitude

Attitude is all about how a person acts, thinks or feels about something, so obviously a player's attitude towards rugby will determine how he plays the game.

Central to a player's attitude is practising and playing the game to the best of his ability — on behalf of himself, his team, the club and any region or country he might represent.

Be professional

Everything he does in rugby, whether he is a schoolboy or a paid professional, he must try to do to the highest standards.

Confidence

He should have confidence in himself and the knowledge that his courage will conquer any fears.

Decision-making

He should know that, as a player, even if he is not the captain, he is still a decision-maker and will be required to make decisions on the field, as necessary, for the benefit of his team.

Effort

He should give the maximum effort at all times and make no excuses. If, after giving of his best, things still go wrong he should not blame himself nor any of his team-mates, but get on with the game.

There's no shortage of attitude with Ireland's Keith Wood. Despite the tackle by Argentina's Gonzalo Longo, Wood will do his utmost to stay on his feet until his support arrives.

Above: In this picture Jonah Lomu exemplifies the attitude of putting all his effort into his game.

Enjoyment

He enjoys his rugby because that is what it's all about: rugby is a game to be enjoyed.

Equipment

He should look after his equipment. That includes his boots (rugby shoes in North America), mouthguard (gumshield), kit, kit bag and any padding or other clothing or accessories he uses for the game.

Health

He should also look after his own body by keeping it fit and taking care to maintain a balanced and healthy diet (not just fast food or junk food).

Referees

He should remember that referees are human. When they make bad decisions the player just has to put it behind him and get on with the game. Make up for it by playing harder.

Sportsmanship

The player should respect the opposition and play fairly against them, but do everything he can during the match to beat them. After the match, win or lose, he behaves sportingly with them and develops friendships.

Below: The normally intense rivalry between the All Blacks and the Wallabies is put aside for now as both teams sportingly acknowledge each other after a hard-fought match.

Gareth Edwards, the former Welsh scrum-half, was voted Britain's rugby player of the 20th century. The Welsh will tell you there was a time when the Welsh team came down with the flu and Gareth had to play England on his own.

One Welsh fan was stuck outside the ground without a ticket. Suddenly, from the other side of the fence he heard a mighty roar. 'What's happening?' he shouted.

'It's ok,' his friend shouted back. 'Gareth just scored.'

7

Specialised Skills

Along with the basic skills, there are two specialised skills in rugby that some players use a lot and some players use only occasionally. They are kicking and tryscoring.

Kicking

Done well, kicking the ball is a good way to make rapid progress up the field or escape from the pressure of an opposition attack. Done badly, or too often, it wastes good possession and becomes too predictable. Kicking should always be done for a reason and it should always be accurate. The three basic types of kick are: **place kick**, **drop kick** and **punt**.

The place kick

When the ball is deliberately placed on the ground, usually upright, and a player runs up to it before kicking it, it is called a place kick. The place kick is used to start a game and to restart it after half time, and to take kicks at goal.

In days gone by, kickers placed the ball in a hole they heeled in the ground and then kicked the ball with the toe of their boot. Nowadays most kickers place the ball on sand or a kicking tee and kick the ball with their instep. The seam of the ball is positioned pointing towards the posts and leaning forward or back as the kicker prefers.

The kicker then takes measured steps backwards away from the ball. He pauses, sights the ball, the posts, and visualises the ball going between them. He should be calm and relaxed, avoiding any distractions.

Perhaps the best kicker in world rugby, Neil Jenkins' body is cocked like a gun. Note the non-kicking foot is placed beside the ball, his kicking foot is fully drawn back and his head is down over the ball.

Left: Adrian Cashmore of the Auckland Blues shows perfect balance as he takes a place kick. Note his left arm is extended to counter-balance his kicking foot.

Below: Andrew Mehrtens is attacking the ball with more aggression, probably because he has to kick the ball a longer distance.

When ready, he runs forward with measured steps, places his non-kicking foot firmly on the ground beside the ball, and swings the kicking leg through an arc to strike the ball just above the ground and send it towards the goalposts.

The boot kicks right 'through' the ball, swinging well past the point of contact.

Place kicks to start the first and second half are similar, except the kicker leans back to try to get under the ball to send it higher, so his forwards will have more chance of getting to it.

Every kick must have a purpose.

The drop kick

This is a specialised kick where the ball is deliberately dropped to the ground and the boot makes contact with the ball immediately

Right: Perfect technique of the drop kick by Joel Stransky (right) and this kick was perfect – it won South Africa the 1995 World Cup.

Below: As Canada's Gareth Rees places the ball on the kicking tee he is already concentrating on the kick.

after it has bounced. The drop kick is used to restart play and for kicks at goal (a field goal). The restarts are taken from the 22-metre line and the half-way line.

In a drop kick the ball is held vertically in both hands at about waist height. The kicker usually takes a single step forward and drops the ball, point downwards and tilted slightly backwards. The kicking foot is drawn backwards at the same time and, a half-second after the ball has bounced, the foot swings forward to strike through the ball with the instep.

For longer kicks the player leans into the ball. To loft the ball at kick restarts, he leans backwards and gets his foot under the ball. This higher kick allows time for his forwards to make ground and to contest possession.

The punt

The punt is the general purpose kick, used when kicking for touch, to make ground, relieve pressure or simply to take the ball beyond the first line of defence. Common to all these is the need to move the ball from your defensive area into an attacking area

Above: Christian Cullen is well balanced to punt the ball upfield, eyes fixed on the ball.

Right: Tana Umaga has dropped the ball onto his foot late to conceal the fact that he is going to kick.

in the opponent's half. If the intention is to keep the ball in play, then the ball should be kicked as far as possible and away from opposing players to make it as difficult as possible for them to launch a counter-attack.

To punt effectively the kicker holds the ball in front of him and drops it a full leg's length away from the body to maximise the swing of the kicking leg. The non-kicking foot is planted firmly on the ground, the kicking foot drawn back behind the body, then swung forward to make contact, using the instep, with the fullest part of the ball. The head and shoulders are bent forward, the eyes fixed on the ball. The kicking foot strikes right through the ball.

Players should practise with both feet as there will not always be time in match situations to rely on their favoured foot.

The chip kick

Instead of trying to beat a tackler or a defensive screen on the ground, the attacker chips the ball over the heads of the defenders. He or his team-mates run through the defensive line to retrieve the ball. This kick is sometimes called the chip-and-chase.

In a well-judged chip kick the ball can be caught by an attacking player before it bounces. If it does bounce, regathering the ball is not always easy, but the chaser should persevere until the ball bounces favourably and can be caught. This often results in a clear run to the goal line, or, if it bounces over the goal line, he can dive on it to score.

The key to the chip kick is timing: when a defender is committed to a tackle or momentarily flat-footed, it is difficult to turn quickly and give chase.

The three kicking essentials are concentration, rhythm and timing.

Below: Innovation from Carlos Spencer, who draws the defence then chips the ball with his knee.

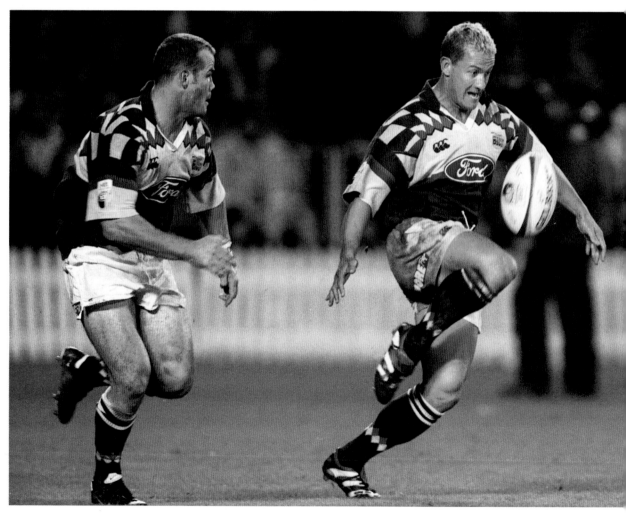

Right: Christian Cullen has timed his chip kick too late. The tackle from Tongan Fepi'kou Tatafu prevents Cullen from chasing the kick himself, though he could be successful if he has committed defenders to cover him and if his team-mates are running through at top speed.

Desperate defence: if in doubt, kick it out.

Kicking to touch

When under sustained pressure *inside* their own 22, many teams will kick directly to touch at the first opportunity. To do this effectively the kicker should try to send the ball directly out of play at a height which is beyond their opponent's reach. The distance gained is important also, but that has to be balanced against the desperateness of the situation.

The ball cannot be kicked directly into touch from *outside* the 22-metre line, so kickers should develop an awareness of where the touchlines are and practise kicks that have the ball crossing the touchline after one or two bounces in the field of play.

The wipers kick

Named after the side-to-side motion of windshield wipers, this is an angled punt across the field in the direction of the open-side corner flag with the purpose of changing the direction of play and wrong-footing the opposition. It is particularly effective when play

Left: The ball is about a leg length away as Carlos Spencer prepares to kick. He has timed the kick exactly right to cause Jeff Wilson to stop dead.

has become massed on one side of the field and the opposition has little defence on the other side. In this situation a wipers kick will often dribble into touch undefended, making good ground and obtaining good field position for the attacking team.

The cross kick

This is similar to the wipers kick except it is flatter and more tactical. It is best used when the attacking side has a numerical advantage out wide; the kick is directed into undefended space where unmarked players of the attacking side can run on to the ball and continue the attack. The cross kick is an almost flat kick in the form of a long chip kick which gets the ball quickly across field.

The screw or spiral kick

The screw kick is a punt in which, rather than kick right through the middle of the ball, the kicker gives it a firm but glancing blow causing it to spin in flight. This reduces air resistance, allowing

Kicking Practice Game

Two players stand opposite each other on a rugby field, each on a 22-metre line. One punts the ball towards the other. If he catches it, he gets to take five paces forward from where he caught it, and kick it back. Otherwise he must kick from where he collected the ball or where it went over the touchline. The idea is, by clever kicking and good catching, to get close enough to your opponent's goalposts to drop kick the ball between them. The first person to succeed with a dropped goal is the winner.

the ball to go further through a flatter trajectory. The screw kick is effective when kicking to touch outside the 22, and also for kicking into a strong wind.

The up-and-under

Also known as the Garryowen (after the Irish club that used it frequently), this is a punt in the opposition's half of the field where the ball is kicked high into the air, just far enough upfield to allow players of the attacking team to contest possession when it comes down. It is sometimes a good attacking option inside the opposition's 22, especially if the fullback is a poor catcher.

The up-and-under is also used when a player is isolated in a defensive position. Then he might kick the ball high over the heads of the opposing team and give chase, putting his team-mates onside as he does so.

The grubber kick

The grubber kick is a punt in which the ball is kicked for a short distance, low along the ground. It is useful when kicking to touch outside the 22. It is also used to kick between defenders for a support player to run on to, similar in purpose to the chip kick. When used in this way it is likely to catch defenders off guard because the kicker does not prepare to take the kick until the last possible moment.

Right: The classic scenario as Andrew Mehrtens makes a clearing kick. The opposition in front of him attempts to block it, while his own player in support, prepares to give chase.

The hack kick

The hack kick is used when the ball is loose on the ground with little chance of claiming it by hand, or it is too risky to attempt a pick-up when the ball is wet. Instead, an advantage might be gained by 'hacking' the ball forward — soccer style — in order to pick it up in more space or with more time, or even hack it again, depending on the circumstances.

The box kick

This is a specialised kick usually used by the scrum-half at a lineout, scrum, maul or ruck. He kicks the ball high into the air in the direction of the opposing blind-side wing. His own wing, usually primed by a signal, sprints forward in an attempt to get to the ball first or put pressure on the opposition wing. The 'box' is the open space in front of the blind-side wing and fullback, and behind the forwards, in a set-play situation.

The over-the-shoulder kick

A version of the box kick in which the scrum-half, chasing backwards to collect a loose ball, back to the opposition, executes a box kick over his shoulder before the opposition forwards can catch him in possession.

Above: Daniel Herbert has kicked ahead too late, meaning he has been wrapped up in the tackle and will not be able to follow his own kick.

Left: When under pressure near your own goal line, a kick does not have to look pretty — as long as you can get it past the opposition and into the safety of touch.

Right: This chip kick has been timed to perfection by Jeff Wilson as he has committed Tim Horan to an attempted block.

Kicking tactics: Though every player in a team should be able to hack kick and punt, most teams have rules and strategies for elected players to kick in specific situations. These players should be positioned accordingly, where they can make the most appropriate kick in the circumstances.

The tap kick

The tap kick is an option when a team has been awarded a penalty kick. Rather than kick for goal or for the touchline, the ball is held in both hands, released, tapped with the foot and immediately regathered by the kicker. The ball is in play again and the kicker can run forward or pass the ball.

Wind effects

When a ball is kicked into the air its course is influenced by the wind. Before a match starts a kicker should check which way the wind is blowing and how strongly. One trick is to throw grass in the air and see which way it blows.

Kickers must use the wind to their team's advantage. When the wind is behind them, especially if it is strong, kickers should kick more frequently, though still wisely.

In 1960 France beat Ireland 23-6 to share the championship with England. Pierre Albaladejo became the first player to kick three dropped goals in an international and was appropriately given the nickname 'Monsieur Le Drop'.

Tryscoring

Everybody knows how to score a try. You hold the ball and fall over the opposition's goal line. Then you get up and shout with delight. Simple. But many tries have been lost because players have not used the proper technique to ground the ball when they are near or over the goal line.

Grounding the ball

The ball must be grounded with downward pressure on or over the opponent's line, using the hands, arms or upper body. If the ball carrier crosses the goal line out wide and there are no defenders close by, he should try and get closer to the posts to make the conversion attempt easier for the kicker.

Low body position

When trying to cross a defended goal line the player should get his body position as low as possible and drive for the line with the ball hugged safely to his chest. He should aim to ground the ball about a ball's length over the line in case the tackler knocks him back a little in the tackle.

When a player is about to be tackled from behind while scoring, he too should keep his body position low to minimise the risk of the ball being jarred out in the tackle.

Don't leave it to chance: make sure you ground the ball properly.

Reaching out

Normally when grounding the ball, a player must keep a firm grip on it. But if tackled just short of the goal line, he is allowed to reach out for the line as long as he does so immediately. When striving to reach the goal line near the corner flag, the feet should be off the ground in the dive to avoid stepping on the touchline. The ball has to be grounded before any part of the tryscorer's body touches the corner flag or the touchline.

This skill should be practised by wingers and others who often score tries near the corner.

Pushover try

A pushover try comes from a scrum in which the attacking team pushes their opponents over the goal line. The No. 8 controls the ball with his feet, keeping it in the scrum until it is on or over the opponent's line, then disengages from the scrum and falls on the ball to score the try.

Penalty try

A penalty try is awarded by the referee when a defending team uses foul play to prevent what he considers would have been a certain try. But the person who would have scored it does not get the credit — it is awarded to the team.

Above: A winger should know his way to the touchline. Gareth Thomas forces his way over, despite being tackled.

Below: What looks like a spectacular try is actually Tana Umaga saving one by touching the ball down in his own in-goal, but the techniques are the same commitment, concentration and fingertip control.

8

Set Play: The Scrum

All players must practise the individual skills appropriate to their playing positions. When these skills are practised with others they become unit and team skills. Rugby is a very structured game which is divided into **set play**, **second phase** and **open play**.

Set play (or a 'set piece') is a way of restarting the game after a stoppage — after a team has scored, for example. Set play includes **scrums**, **lineouts**, **kick restarts** and **penalties**.

Second phase (chapter 12) is where the ball is contested in tackle situations, rucks and mauls. In the modern game teams will deliberately set up a ruck or a maul to draw in defenders and regain possession of the ball before launching an attack.

Open play is the term used when play continues uninterrupted by the referee for a significant period of time. Often fast and exciting, open play rarely lasts for more than a few minutes at a time.

Scrums

The scrum is sometimes referred to as the engine room — the source of the power which drives the whole team. Therefore, success or failure in the scrum *affects* the whole team. The ability of the scrum to apply and absorb pressure influences the rucks and mauls which follow it. For example, if a team has possession of the ball in the scrum and is going forward, it is easier for them to launch an attack. But if its forwards buckle under pressure, then the quality of possession will be poor and an attack will be less likely to succeed.

A good scrum consists of all eight forwards working together as individuals, as units within the scrum and as a complete pack. A good scrum is a tightly bound, concentrated and disciplined unit, with each player having a different role to play.

The forwards must follow the referee's instructions before engaging the scrum.

The front row

The whole scrum is like a blunt-nosed battering ram trying to force the opposition backwards. The front row is the face of that battering ram, not only having to push forward but also able to support their own players pushing from behind.

The formation of the front row starts with the hooker. When preparing to set the scrum he raises his arms so that a prop on each side can tuck a shoulder underneath; the hooker then grips each prop by their jersey. In the same way each prop puts his nearest arm around the back of the hooker so that all three are tightly bound together.

At this point, the weight of the front row should be leaning slightly backwards to counter the weight of the second row and the back row that are joining the scrum behind them. The legs of the front row are splayed slightly outwards, their knees slightly bent, their backs straight. They look straight into the eyes of the opposing front row. They should be mentally prepared for the impact when the referee sets the scrum. Their intention is to move forward, shunting the other team backward.

Above: The All Black front row is tightly bound, set low and looks ready for engagement with their Australian counterparts.

The second row

If the scrum is the engine room then the second row is the boiler room. Because they are bound in the middle of the scrum and because they are able to lean forward with their whole body length (unlike the props) they give the scrum most of its forward push. Before they join with the front row, the second rowers bind with each other in similar fashion to the front row — by linking arms around each other's backs. Each second row forward then places his innermost shoulder against the hooker's thighs and the other shoulder against his prop. He grips the prop with his free hand.

Right: Note the low body position and tight binding of the Wellington Hurricanes' second row and front row at scrum practice. The backs are straight and the legs slightly bent ready to push.

The back row

The two flankers place their inside shoulders against the outside buttocks of the two props. They should push straight even though they are on the side of the scrum.

The No. 8 puts his shoulders up against the buttocks of the two second row forwards in front of him. His arms go around their hips. He will be leaning full length like the second row.

The scrum is now set and ready for engagement.

Above: A wider shot shows the All Black scrum at training, though the flanker on the left side of the picture seems to have come up a little high. Note the concentration on the faces of those watching. Those in the scrum should be even more concentrated.

The engagement

The front row now takes on a crouching position. They should be low, but the shoulders no lower than the hips. They will be about one metre away from the opposing forwards. When the referee tells the two sets of forwards to engage, the two front rows impact against each other, heads interlocking, those of the two loosehead props remaining on the outside.

The players in the scrum should keep their backs straight and their legs slightly flexed ready to push as soon as the scrum-half puts the ball into the scrum. The scrum-half will often alert his own team by a coded call when the ball is about to be put in so that they can get a start on the other team. This co-ordination between the scrum-half and the front row should be practised in training. The scrum-half should feed the ball into the scrum at a slight angle to make it easier for his own hooker to hook it back on his side.

Below: The front rows of the New South Wales Waratahs and the Otago Highlanders are set at different heights, but both look ready and are eyeballing each other as the referee holds them apart.

Strength, technique and courage decide who wins the pushing contest of the scrum. Lack of courage in the front row will be noticed by the opposing front row and exploited as a weakness — as will a lack of technique anywhere among the forwards.

If one team is obviously stronger in the scrums, then that team will have an advantage and attempt to roll the other team backwards at every opportunity. This tires out the opposing forwards, gains territory and forces the opposing backs to retreat.

The channels

The ball is put into the scrum by the scrum-half. When the ball has been won by the hooker, the forwards have to channel the ball to the back of the scrum where the scrum-half or No. 8 can pick it up. No one else is allowed to touch the ball until it has been cleared from the scrum.

There are three basic channels. The first is between the prop and the left flanker. This is not very safe because the opposing scrum-half will be hovering there waiting to pounce. A safer channel is between the two locks and back to the No. 8 who gets the ball on his right side, his bulk protecting it from the opposing scrum-half. A third channel brings the ball out between the right-hand lock and the right-hand flanker. This is safer again, but harder to achieve because it is farthest away from the side the ball was put in.

Kit Bag for the Junior Footballer

Motto:
Be better prepared than your opponent.

Checklist:
• Mouthguard (which minimises concussion and dental injury — always carry a spare)
• shin pads
• boots
• tape (for taping the laces so they don't come undone)
• protective padding
• training gear
• wet weather tracksuits
• woolly hat
• thermal vests.

Left: George Gregan, knees bent, leaning forward, puts the ball into the ACT Brumbies scrum.

Right: Kevin Dalzell of the USA clears. The maul or ruck behind him is a mess with many players off balance and off their feet.

The defensive scrum

The defensive scrum is almost the same as the attacking scrum. No matter who has the ball, both sets of forwards are trying to win the pushing contest. But as the ball moves back towards the channel, the loose forwards of the defending team should raise their heads (remaining bound as the law demands) to see what the opposition is going to do with it.

As the tight forwards cannot always see when the ball has come free of the scrum, one of the loose forwards has the job of shouting to them when to break.

Scrum practice

When practising scrummaging, coaches and players should spend time getting techniques exactly right, getting the feet exactly right, getting the back straight. If the basic techniques are perfected at an early age, players will scrummage correctly and safely all their lives. As soon as the basic techniques are mastered, weight and opposition can be added. Scrummaging should be practised both on a scrum machine and against real opponents.

> Noel Murphy, coach of the 1980 British Lions to South Africa often got speeches muddled— "Right lads, I want 80% commitment for 100 minutes!" Murphy also invented a revolutionary tactic when he said, "Right lads, spread out in a bunch."

9

Set Play: The Lineout

The line

The lineout is a set way of getting the ball back into play after it has gone over the touchline. The team to touch it last is deemed to have taken it out of play and the other team gets to throw it back in (except when the ball is kicked out from a penalty).

The two sets of forwards line up about a metre apart. The jumpers are usually the tallest players and the other players support them. The main jumpers normally stand at 2, 4 and 6, but this can be varied by the team throwing in.

The throw

These days it is the hooker who usually throws in the ball, athough this too can be varied. The ball can be propelled in any way as long as it goes in a straight line between the two rows of forwards. Most hookers take the ball back behind their head with both hands and then throw it forward with one or both hands. It has to go at least five metres.

The code

Before the ball is thrown in, the attacking team will decide which of their jumpers should catch it and what subsequent move they will attempt. One player — one of the forwards or the scrum-half — will have the job of making the lineout calls. He tells the other players by calling out the move in a code. Such a code might be a 'magic number', decided before the game, which is used to precede the jumper's position in the lineout. For example, if the magic number is '3' then a call of '132' would mean the ball will be thrown towards the jumper standing at number 2; a call of '34' would be

John Tait of Canada uses his inside arm to catch the ball in this lineout against Fiji.

aimed at jumper number four. The code should be repeated as necessary to make sure every player on the attacking team hears it. They should also have a back-up code in case the opposing team is able to crack the first one.

Above: Todd Blackadder (centre) looks like he is about to get the ball at the lineout after a signal to his thrower.

There is also a coded communication between the hooker and the jumper. The hooker can throw the ball flat or looped, quickly or delayed. He will signal his intentions to the jumper by using body language — twitches, raised eyebrows or even the way he stands — and the jumper might respond in similar ways to indicate how he would like to receive the ball. These signals, of course, are previously agreed on and practised in training.

The hooker must throw the ball so that the jumper will catch it at the top of his jump (unless a flat throw has been called).

The jump

The jumper must jump off both feet and be aggressive in trying to catch the ball. He must be prepared for his opposite to obstruct him, and he must time his jump so that he can take the ball cleanly.

There are three basic jumps he can do. He can jump forward into the ball; he can jump straight into the air, or he can jump

Above: A good throw has Norm Maxwell at full stretch when he takes this ball, meaning the opposition is less likely to reach it.

backwards to take a looped throw from the hooker. If there is space, he can also take steps forward or backward.

As soon as he jumps, the props and/or other supporting players hold him up in the air so that he has more 'hang time' and therefore more chance of catching the ball. As soon as he has got it, he must twist towards his own team to keep the ball away from the opposition. As he lands, the supporting players must form a wedge either side of him so that the opposition is unable to get at the ball. He should then hold on to the ball until instructed to release it by the scrum-half.

Variations on the lineout

The one-handed tap back

If the jumper can't get two hands on the ball he should try to tap it back on to his side with his inside hand. (Using the outside arm is illegal and will give away a penalty.) An accurate tap back gets

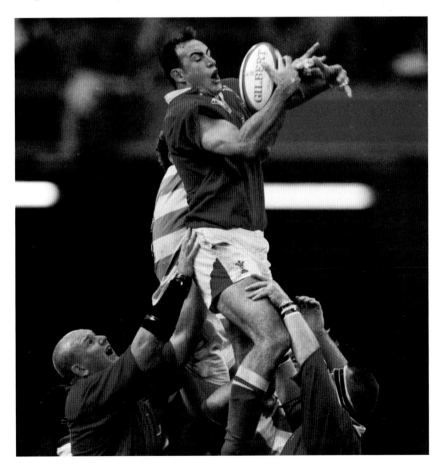

Right: Wales' Chris Wyatt shows the aggression and concentration needed to attack the ball at the lineout.

the ball back to the scrum-half quicker and can set up an immediate attack. However, a wild, one-handed tap back that does not go straight to the scrum-half often presents an advantage to the opposition who come chasing through after it. This is particularly dangerous in wet weather with a slippery ball.

The shortened lineout

A normal lineout consists of the seven forwards from each side. The team throwing in the ball decides how many are to comprise the lineout. Fewer than seven and the lineout is considered shortened. If the defending team uses more players than the attacking team they will be penalised (if the referee or touch judges spot it).

A shortened lineout must have at least two players from each side and may be preferred for several reasons: perhaps the team throwing in is losing a lot of ball at the normal lineouts; perhaps it has a better jumper who will have more space in which to jump in a shortened lineout, or it might be to initiate a special move with the forwards not part of the lineout. And so on.

Above: In this competitive lineout David Hodges of the USA seems to have won the contest against Ireland's Dion O'Cuinnegain.

Changing positions

The main jumpers can be moved around in the lineout to take up other positions. If jumpers in the attacking team change position in the lineout, then those jumpers marking them should also move to that position.

Adding a man

The attacking team does not have to announce how many men are to stand in the lineout — that is decided by the player who does the lineout calls. It is up to the defending team to count them and make sure they have the same number. Just before the ball is thrown in, a member of the attacking team can rejoin the lineout to become a new (unopposed) jumper.

The throw over the top

The ball must be thrown straight down the gap formed between the two sets of forwards, but it can also be thrown straight over the top of them with a long and accurate throw. This would be a called move and a player from the attacking team, who was not in the lineout, would come forward from a deep position to take it. But the throw must be straight.

Right: Danny Grewcock has climbed high and released the ball at the top of his jump to give his scrum-half more time to pass it.

The quick throw-in

The team which has the throw-in can throw the ball in even before a lineout is formed. Any player in that team can take the throw-in as long as he is the only person to have touched the ball outside the field of play. The quick throw-in must be straight and taken from a position level with or behind where the ball went into touch. A player is even allowed to throw the ball in and catch it himself, but he must be sure to throw it over the five-metre line.

The quick throw-in is generally used in two situations. One is where the team that has the throw-in is on attack. The thrower sees a player on his own team in a good position and the defending team momentarily disorganised. A quick throw-in, especially if it is near the defending team's line, can catch them off guard and may result in a try.

A quick throw-in can also be taken on defence when the attacking team has kicked the ball far down field and there are no chasers to prevent the defending team taking an unopposed throw.

Left: Despite the pressure from the Australian jumper, All Black Robin Brooke has jumped aggressively to win the ball at the front of the lineout. Note how he has turned towards his own side to protect the ball.

Right: Taine Randell has climbed high at the back of the lineout and released the ball early. In this situation forwards can peel around from the front of the lineout and take the ball up behind the tail of the lineout.

Basic moves from the lineout

The peel

The ball is thrown into the lineout. The prop or another player peels off the front of the lineout and runs back between the line-out and the scrum-half. The catcher, instead of passing the ball to the scrum-half, deflects it to the prop who makes a charge along the end of the line into the opposition forwards or backs.

The blind-side charge

This is similar to the last move except this time the hooker, after throwing the ball into the lineout, stays on the blind side (the five-metre gap between the front of the lineout and the touchline). The ball is thrown back to him (or another attacking player) by the successful jumper in the lineout and he then charges through the gap, running parallel with the touchline.

The wing comes in

The lineout ball is won and the wing cuts back from his wing (on the side where the lineout takes place) to take the ball near the end of the line and charge at an angle towards the opposition backs.

Defending a lineout

Nowadays, teams sometimes choose not to compete in lineouts where lifting makes it easier for the team throwing in the ball to win it. In this case the defending team should concentrate solely on stopping any forward drive by the opposition.

When a jumper in the defending team does compete, he should usually attempt a one-handed tap back. Players in the defending team should also try to burst through any gaps in the attacking team's lineout to get to the ball, catch the scrum-half in possession or just to put pressure on the opposing team.

Defending jumpers, when leaping for the ball, should always do so aggressively; even if they don't get a hand to the ball their actions will help to spoil the other team's possession.

The defending team's hooker should be marking his opposite when he throws the ball in. He should stay in that position immediately after the ball has been thrown in, ready to block any blind-side move by the opposing team.

Above: Pat Dunkley of Canada holds the ball behind his head to throw it into the lineout.

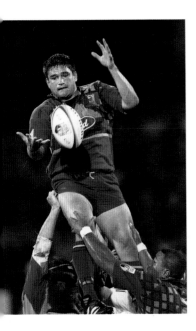

107

10

Set Play: Kick Restarts

The kick-off

At the kick-off, all members of the kicker's team should be behind the kicker. The forwards group together on one side to chase the ball as soon as it has been kicked.

The ball must be kicked over the ten-metre line or the opposing team will get a scrum back on the halfway line. Before he kicks the ball, the kicker should signal to his own team the kind of kick they can expect: whether he is going to kick the ball just over the ten-metre line or deep towards the opposing 22, near the touchline or away from the touchline.

One or two of the fastest forwards should be the main chasers, their job is to get to the ball first and secure possession. To achieve this they should time their run from well behind the kicker to be almost at full speed when they come level with him.

The 22-metre drop-out

This drop kick is similar to the restart from the halfway line after a try has been scored, except it has to be taken anywhere behind the 22-metre line. The hooker of the opposing team and one other player usually try to obstruct the kicker or charge down the ball, but they are not allowed to cross the 22-metre line.

The kicker can drop kick the ball high into the air for his own forwards to run on to and claim back or he can kick it long down the field. The wingers of the opposing team should stand back at about the halfway line waiting for this long kick.

Defending against a tap penalty

Once a referee has awarded a penalty, a frequent mistake of the defending team is to drop their heads with disappointment, lose

The Blues' Orene Ai'i attempts a long drop-out from the 22.

10

Set Play: Kick Restarts

The kick-off

At the kick-off, all members of the kicker's team should be behind the kicker. The forwards group together on one side to chase the ball as soon as it has been kicked.

The ball must be kicked over the ten-metre line or the opposing team will get a scrum back on the halfway line. Before he kicks the ball, the kicker should signal to his own team the kind of kick they can expect: whether he is going to kick the ball just over the ten-metre line or deep towards the opposing 22, near the touchline or away from the touchline.

One or two of the fastest forwards should be the main chasers, their job is to get to the ball first and secure possession. To achieve this they should time their run from well behind the kicker to be almost at full speed when they come level with him.

The 22-metre drop-out

This drop kick is similar to the restart from the halfway line after a try has been scored, except it has to be taken anywhere behind the 22-metre line. The hooker of the opposing team and one other player usually try to obstruct the kicker or charge down the ball, but they are not allowed to cross the 22-metre line.

The kicker can drop kick the ball high into the air for his own forwards to run on to and claim back or he can kick it long down the field. The wingers of the opposing team should stand back at about the halfway line waiting for this long kick.

Defending against a tap penalty

Once a referee has awarded a penalty, a frequent mistake of the defending team is to drop their heads with disappointment, lose

The Blues' Orene Ai'i attempts a long drop-out from the 22.

Above: The Australian player is allowed to be in front of the kicker because he is placing the ball on a windy day.

concentration or even turn their backs. Even though the referee has blown his whistle, the game has stopped only long enough for the penalty to be taken, and if they wish, the team given the penalty can take a quick tap kick immediately.

As soon as a penalty has been awarded, defending players still on their feet should retire the regulation ten metres to be prepared for the quick tap. Those who are on the ground should get to their feet as quickly as possible and do the same.

Even if a tap kick is not taken, losing ground by conceding the penalty is almost inevitable and a disciplined team will retire and regroup as fast as possible.

Defending against the forward charge from a tap penalty

A team will often use a tap penalty to start a forward charge in order to gain ground before the ball is released for a second phase attack.

To counter this, the defending forwards should face their opposites, lined up about one metre apart. The best tackler among them should be in the middle, ready to take the ball carrier. Either side of him should be the strongest players — the front row. The loosies should be on the outside of the line up ready to take off if the attacking team decides to spread the ball out wide.

As soon as the attacking team has taken the tap penalty, the defending players can rush forward to make the tackle. But they must make sure they remain in a line so that no gaps appear.

If the tap penalty is taken ten metres from the defender's goal line, the defending team must definitely charge forward to meet the attackers.

It is essential that when a player gives away a penalty, heads do not go down; rather, the offending team should quickly reset its defence, ready to win back the advantage.

Penalty kick at goal

The defenders must stand at least ten metres back from a penalty kick at goal and are not allowed to charge. One or more of the team's kickers should be positioned near the posts ready to kick the ball to touch if the penalty attempt fails and the ball falls short of the goal line.

If an unsuccessful penalty kick goes over the goal line the usual option is for a defending player to force the ball down for a 22-metre drop-out. Sometimes the catcher might choose to run the ball back into the field of play before kicking to touch (from inside his own 22) or he might link up with other members of his team to create an attacking move.

The conversion

Defending against a conversion is the same as for a penalty kick at goal except that the defending team must stand behind the goal line. Players are only allowed to charge once the kicker starts his run.

Below: As David Holwell takes this kick, his fellow Hurricanes' player at right is onside behind him. The player who conceded the penalty should be in a defensive position ready to clear the ball or counter-attack if the kick misses.

In 1969 Jean-Pierre Salut was selected as the open-side flanker for a French team to play Scotland. The match venue was Stade Colombes, Paris. The changing rooms were under the main grandstand and the players had to run down the corridor and up some stairs to reach the playing ground. Salut, the last man in the French side, tripped on the top step and broke his ankle. He remains the only national player ever to be carried from the field before he actually stepped on it.

111

11

Second Phase

The hallmark of modern rugby is an ability to retain possession for long periods of time. The team which can keep the ball the longest is more likely to score — you can't score *without* the ball.

Between the disciplines of set play and the excitement of open rugby is the close-quarter stuff known as second phase rugby. Whenever play breaks down possession is disputed. It might be a simple tackled ball situation, a ruck or a maul. (The difference between a ruck and a maul is that in a ruck the ball is on the ground, while in a maul the ball is to hand.) In each case, however, the side which had possession at the breakdown is trying to regain the ball to launch a second phase attack. The other team, of course, is trying to 'steal' it, or 'turn it over'.

Tackled ball

In most situations the player with the ball knows when he is about to be tackled. Sometimes he might slip the tackle with speed or deception, but when it's clear he's going to be held up he should decide how best to take the tackle and how to ensure his team retains possession of the ball.

If it's not possible to pass the ball to a supporting team-mate he must elect to either remain on his feet or go to the ground. This decision depends on several factors, such as his strength, the relative size of his tackler, how many of his team are in support, how many of the opposition are close by and so on, but whatever the situation he must do his best to present the ball back to his own team and use his body to shield the ball from the opposition team. If he stays on his feet, he should try to half turn towards his team-mates. If players bind on him a maul is formed.

Jonah Lomu is taken low by these French players and looks as though he'll fall. Several French players are well placed to compete for the ball.

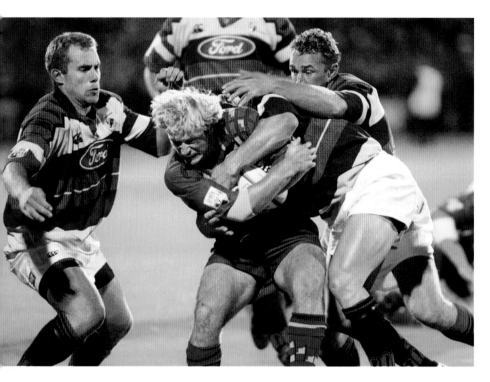

Left: Tony Brown has been collared by the Canterbury defence and if he succeeds in staying on his feet a maul will form.

The maul

The supporting players to arrive must first form a wedge around the tackled player by supporting him on each side and shielding the ball from the opposition. Others do the same, widening the wedge to provide a screen which will prevent the opposition from getting anywhere near the ball. This is the key to retaining possession. Players can join in a maul on their own side as long as they come from behind the hindmost feet — they are not allowed to come around the maul. If the binding is solid and tight, the opposition forwards will be unable to get at the ball.

When a tackle is made in the backline and the forwards are slow to arrive, the backs must engage in the maul to form a wedge that will keep the opposition away from the ball. Backs should practice this in training.

Sometimes the first player to arrive will take the ball off the tackled player and a maul might form around him.

Ripping or stripping the ball

Often a maul is part formed with an opposition player still wrestling for the ball. In this case he should be driven back or squeezed away from the ball.

Below: Fabien Galthie of France cuts through the Argentine defence. He looks like he will get tackled, but has players in support to form the ruck or maul and France should retain the ball.

Right: This looks like a tackled ball situation. England wing Dan Luger has his hands around Jonah Lomu, but Lomu broke the tackle and went on to score.

When trying to wrestle the ball from another player, or the ball is trapped and needs to be 'stripped' from the maul, more aggressive action is sometimes required. Shape up as though going for the ball with both hands but use the force of the whole body, shoulder first, to thrust one hand downwards 'through' the ball.

The driving maul

The purpose of the maul is to secure possession, but if the maul is going forward the attacking side — usually instructed by their scrum-half — might decide to continue driving forward to gain ground. The ball should be carried by a player in the second row of the maul to protect it from the opposition. In a maul of this kind the first line of forwards may stand upright, but those behind should adopt a low body position to push the maul forward. The drive should be continued for as long as the maul is moving forward. Once the maul becomes stationary a change of tactics must be employed: either the ball is released to the scrum-half or it is moved to other players in a position to continue progress with a rolling maul. Failure to make use of the ball once the maul has stopped going forward may result in the referee stopping play and handing possession to the other side.

Left: A strong forward drive from Wales' prop Peter Rogers breaks through the Samoan defence. His team-mates in support should be able to keep the momentum going if he falls to the ground.

The rolling maul

This is similar to the driving maul, except that when the maul has become stationary, the attacking team smuggles the ball across to the side of the maul where the defence seems weakest (the ball must always travel backwards of course). The player rolls out to the side, tightly supported by his team-mates. As soon as the new unit makes ground, the other forwards peel off the older part of the maul and support the new movement.

As the defending team regroups and 'plugs the gap' the ball is again smuggled to another part of the maul to change the point of attack. A rolling maul can continue indefinitely in this way but the attacking team must not continue it too long and risk losing the ball.

The rolling maul should be co-ordinated by the scrum-half who has the best view of what is going on. He should be talking to his forwards continuously, telling them where the defence is weakest and instructing other players where to support. The best line of attack in a rolling maul is often the side opposite to where the ball originally came from.

A rolling maul can be a very effective try-scoring manoeuvre from a lineout near the opponent's line and if done well is very difficult to stop.

Right: Ben Tune of Australia has gone to the ground and must immediately release or place the ball. South Africa's Pieter Rossouw has stayed on his feet and is allowed to play the ball.

Below: Ruck or maul? It all depends whether Mark Taylor manages to stay on his feet. The two closest Argentine players are temporarily out of the game because they are off their feet.

The ruck

A ruck is a loose scrum formed in open play. The original meaning of the word ruck is 'a heap of things' and so a ruck came to mean a heap of bodies all trying to get the ball off the ground.

The modern ruck was formed in the 1940s when Vic Cavanagh, coach of the Otago team in New Zealand, organised his forwards into a sort of loose scrum which drove over the loose ball. From there the technique spread all over the world as a faster way of gaining possession of the ball than from a maul situation. This speed gives the attackers an extra advantage as the defenders do not have time to regroup.

The start of the ruck

A ruck is formed when at least two opposing players are in contact with each other over a loose ball on the ground. As soon as a ruck is formed it is illegal to use the hands to control or repossess the ball. The feet must be used to hook the ball back or the players can drive forward and step over the ball so that it comes out on their side.

117

Left: South Africa's Robbie Fleck looks like he'll be wrapped up by the Australian defence, but how quickly will the other Australian players get back to their own side to contest the ruck or maul that forms?

Right: Keith Lowen of the Auckland Blues has been caught by two Wellington Hurricanes. All players are off balance and will get to their feet before they can play the ball again.

Creating the ruck

In the modern game players often deliberately initiate a ruck by falling to the ground in, or just prior to, the tackle. They lie with their body shielding the ball from the opposition, thus making it easier for their own team to regain possession. The player who has fallen to the ground is allowed to place the ball on the ground or push it towards his own team, as long as he does it *immediately* and does not hang on to the ball. The ruck is formed as players from both sides converge on the loose ball.

The first wave of support players from the attacking team should drop their shoulders and bind together like a scrum, a pace or two before they hit the ruck. With short pumping steps, they will attempt to step over the player and the ball and drive back the opposition players.

Other players — usually the slower forwards — join in. The secrets to success are in the low body position (shoulders level with, or just a little higher than, the hips) and all participants being tightly bound (they should be so close together that you could throw a blanket over them).

A ruck can be a source of fast attacking possession. The key to a ruck is low body position and tight binding.

Right: Matt Burke seems to have slipped the tackle of Cristophe Lamaison in the 1999 World Cup final, but John Eales (left) is poised in support if the move breaks down.

A ruck is not really a pushing contest like a scrum. The team's forwards that form up and start driving first are almost always the ones who will win the ruck.

Sometimes the ball becomes lodged in the ruck behind bodies that are in the way and an attacking team needs to dig the ball out with their feet. Sometimes a player on the ground is blocking the ball from coming out. He, too, can be rolled out of the way using the boot in a manner that does not injure him. Do this with care as referees have different interpretations of this technique.

If opposing forwards are hanging on to the side of the ruck, the attacking players in the ruck can bind on them and pull them into the ruck, so preventing them from spoiling the ball as soon as it is freed.

If the first wave of forwards has control of the ruck, then those arriving on the scene a little late should not enter the ruck but

Above: Neil Jenkins tackles Argentina's Octavio Bartolucci. Both are temporarily on the ground, but the two other Welsh players are on their feet and can compete for the ball.

position themselves back, ready to take a pop pass from the scrum-half or to support an attack by the backs.

As in a maul, the ruck should be controlled by the scrum-half, who has the best view of it.

Clearing a ruck

Because ruck ball is fast, attacking ball, the scrum-half must also clear the ball fast or the advantage will be lost. Sometimes he will spread the ball quickly out to the backs who can time their runs better because they can see the ball coming. Sometimes he will just pop it up to forwards who will charge forward and set up the next ruck or maul. If the opposition forwards are in disarray, a series of rucks can be continued down the field.

Because of the nature of the ruck, the scrum-half may not always be available to pass the ball (he might still be at the bottom of the last ruck), so any player in the attacking team must be prepared to act as scrum-half when the ball pops out of the ruck.

Right: Joe Roff has a good, low, driving position, but he has been caught by a French player and looks set to fall to the ground to form a ruck.

Below: In this tackled ball situation Australia's Stephen Larkham seems to have the advantage over Wales' Mark Taylor, but Taylor may force him to pass or form a ruck or maul.

Pick-and-go

Pick-and-go is a fast and specialised form of rucking where an attacking player, obstructed by a defender, goes to the ground and forms a ruck. Several of his team-mates then drive any opposition players off the ball, leaving the ball on the ground behind them (this is called 'blowing over'). Another forward then picks up the ball and goes forward to create the next ruck in the same way. The process is then repeated, often several more times, if it is working and gaining ground.

One of the most famous lineouts of all time, which was labelled by J.B.G. Thomas in the *Western Mail* as the 'Lineout of Shame', was the final lineout of the All Blacks versus Wales game at Cardiff Arms Park in 1978. Andy Haden allegedly dived out of the lineout to secure a last-minute penalty. Haden had walked over to Graham Mourie, who was alongside the injured Doug Bruce, and said quietly in his ear 'I am going to dive. Shall I?' The penalty resulted. However, the referee Roger Quittenton advised the public after the game the penalty wasn't awarded for Haden's dive but against a Welsh player jumping off Frank Oliver's shoulder to launch himself towards the ball, thus breaking the lineout laws.

12

Defence

Defence is based on systems, of which there are three basic types in modern rugby: **man-on-man**, **drift defence** and **man-out defence**. There are many variations and teams will invent new ones for specific situations, such as defending a move off the back of the scrum near their own line. But any plan should be simple and a team should stick to the one they practise. It is crucial that every player in the team is aware of the pattern used and sticks to it in the pressure of a match situation. If any player decides to change it in the middle of a game, holes will appear.

The three major components of a defensive plan are:

1. Marking When in defensive mode every player in the team is responsible for tracking a member of the opposing team — not necessarily his opposite number. He is expected to tackle that player when he gets the ball. That means covering him and staying with him, almost like a mirror image, then quickly closing him down when he is about to receive the ball. If players are well marked, it stifles the options a team has on attack, and perhaps forces them to abandon certain moves.

2. Tackling Every player in the team should make his tackles count.

3. Communication Situations can change rapidly in rugby. An attacking side can change its angles, run decoys and use all sorts of deceptive ploys to baffle the opposition. The defence, therefore, must have systems of communication in place which allow an organised and solid defence to operate successfully. Short sharp code phrases such as 'go out' or 'your man' etc., let players know who is doing what, who is going to tackle whom, and help to maintain the defensive line.

Daniel Herbert has tried to cut back between Wales' fly-half Neil Jenkins and flanker Colin Charvis, but encounters solid defence as Jenkins goes low and Charvis high.

Left: Tana Umaga's dreadlocks fly as he meets the tight Australian defence without a hair's breadth between the tacklers.

Man-on-man defence

In man-on-man defence the players of a defending team tackle their opposite player. But, if the fullback enters the line then the inside player nearest him takes him. There is also a variation of man-on-man defence where the open-side flanker takes the fly-half, especially when his own fly-half is not a good tackler. After that each player takes his own man.

Drift defence

In drift defence the open-side flanker comes off the scrum or the back of the lineout to challenge the opposing fly-half. The defending team's fly-half then takes the opposing team's inside centre. So the defending team's players are not taking the player opposite them, but the next one out and they therefore have to 'drift' across field to make the tackle.

This angle of drifting pushes the attacking team sideways across the field towards the touchline, giving them less space to work in. It also allows for an extra man in the defensive team to take the fullback if he enters the line. This would normally be the outside centre but if the fullback comes into the line in another position, one of the other players would have to tackle him, the players outside having to make adjustments to the defensive line.

Above: New Zealand's Royce Willis has managed to evade South Africa's van der Westhuizen (right) but Fleck makes the tackle.

Man-out defence

In man-out defence, instead of marking opposites from the scrum *outwards*, the defensive pattern starts marking men from the wing *inwards*, towards the scrum.

Blind-side defence

The key to blind-side defence is the early tackle which stops an opposition charge up the blind side. This is the responsibility first of the blind-side flanker, supported by the scrum-half and No. 8. The scrum-half should be communicating with his back row as soon as he sees the opposition shaping up to make a blind-side attack.

The defending winger on the blind side should usually hang back marking his own winger, but if the other defenders are slow or if he sees the need or reads the move early, he can rush in and make the tackle. If he does this he has to make sure the tackle will be successful before he starts his run or he will leave a huge gap for the opposition to run through.

> Ewen Ray Gravell, considered by many to be one of the hardest British tacklers ever, described one of the fundamentals of tackling: 'Get your first tackle in early,' he said, 'even though it may be late.'

13

Attack

The most exciting part of rugby is attack and the ultimate aim when attacking is to score tries. Attacking plans should be innovative and based on the strengths of the personnel in the team. The attacking team should have several moves they can use in a match, but their attacks should also be unpredictable and difficult for the opposition to read.

Attacks should be launched towards open space; if that space becomes defended, another attack should be launched into the new space that is created as a consequence. Generally the most space is to be found at the edges of the field. There are three basic parts to an attacking move: they are the roles played by the **pivot**, the **penetrator** and the **supporters**.

The pivot or playmaker is the player who creates the time or space to launch the attack.

The penetrator is the player who 'penetrates' or breaks through the opposition's defensive line.

The supporters are all the other players in the attacking team who are assisting the attack.

The supporters often do the build-up work, wearing away the opposition defence and committing them to tackles or rucks and mauls. Then the pivot — with a dummy, a delayed pass, or any other deceptive ploy — sets up a situation in which the penetrator is able to take advantage of a gap to run through at speed.

The penetrator's job is to break the line, to get past the initial defence. He will not always be the tryscorer. As soon as he has broken through, the supporters must back him up.

Generally, midfield backs are used as pivots or penetrators. They endeavour to break through the line or create enough space to put their wings away.

Any player can be a penetrator — Wallaby flanker Owen Finigan makes the break against France in the World Cup final.

Above: Pace, aggression and a searing side-step from Glen Osborne take him through the Italian defence.

The back three (the wings and the fullback) are usually used as penetrators. When the fullback comes into the line, he should be running fast to maximise his chances of breaking through.

Any player in a team who is skilled enough can act as a pivot or penetrator when the situation presents itself. Similarly, any player in the attacking team can be used as a distractor, to disguise where the real attack is coming from, usually by decoy runs.

Quality ball

Quality ball is a relative term given to the kind of possession won, generally from a set-piece situation such as a scrum or lineout (though it could also refer to a ruck or maul). Good quality ball is when the ball is freed to the scrum-half quickly and cleanly, allowing him sufficient time and space to weigh up the options and launch the next attack. Poor quality ball is when it comes back untidily and places the attacking side under pressure. Called moves should be cancelled when poor quality ball means the move has little chance of success. One tactic is to start again — create another ruck or maul, set up second-phase possession and deliver

Above: Justin Marshall sees a gap in the South African defence and penetrates with pace.

better quality ball. When the regained ball is of extremely poor quality, the only option is to kick. Teams should have a cancellation call for stopping a move due to poor quality ball.

Breaking the line

Rugby is a physical game, but it is also a thinking game and the smartest team usually wins. When launching an attack, the first object is to break through the opponent's defensive line, to make ground quickly towards their goal line and to have more attacking players in support than there are defenders. Players should also be prepared to use their creative flair and improvisation to break down an opposition defence, though there are several simple moves that all teams use:

The **miss-out** or **cut-out pass** is when a player in the attacking line is bypassed, spreading the ball wider more quickly.

The **scissors** or **cut-back pass** is when the ball carrier cuts across in front of one of his own players and then twists to pass it back to him (the lines of the two players crossing each other are like the

129

blades of an open pair of scissors). The player who now has the ball effectively changes the angle of attack.

An **overlap** is created when the attacking team outnumbers the opposing defence, allowing the 'extra' man to get through (or past) without a tackler to oppose him.

A **loop** is a way of creating an extra man. The ball carrier passes the ball, then runs around behind the receiver to take another pass.

Pick-up from the scrum. The No. 8 picks up the ball from the scrum and breaks towards the blind or open side, supported by his scrum-half and the nearest flanker.

A **blind-side attack** is a very useful way of gaining a territorial advantage, especially when there is a wide blind side, and particularly when attacking down the side opposite to where the ball was put into the scrum (where the opposing scrum-half will be standing). If the attackers can get wide of the blind-side flanker, they have only the wing to beat in the first line of defence.

Below: Daryl Gibson sidesteps through the French defence. At right (partly hidden) is an All Black coming through in support. Pace and support are essential to keep the attack going.

Above: To'o Vaega steps on the gas to get behind the Scottish defence and set up an attacking opportunity for Manu Samoa.

Decoy runs are ways of deceiving the opposition on the point of attack. For example, when planning a blind-side move the attacking fullback can make an open-side run as if he were expecting the ball to be coming his way. This is often just enough to wrong-foot the defence and provide the pivot with that moment of time to gain an advantage.

The **fullback coming into the line** is an excellent way of creating the extra man, changing the angle of the attack or increasing the pace of the attack.

The **wing coming into the line** has the same effect as the full-back coming into the line: he comes off his wing into a new position in the line to create an extra man.

Changing the angle of attack is one of the most effective methods of disrupting a defence. A typical example is the outside centre running out of space, changing direction towards the corner, then

131

passing to his wing who will cut in behind him and head for the goalposts. The wing is effectively wrong-footing the defence which is committed to cutting off the centre. Any combination of players can be used to change the angle of attack.

Communication is as important on attack as on defence. Players call moves and also instruct their team-mates to come in for a pass, move out to receive one or run forward for kicks.

Counter-attack

A **counter-attack** is a quick response to an opposition attack after the attacking team has lost possession of the ball. Sometimes it is safer to kick the ball to touch, but just as often, if the defending team has got players of genuine pace and the other team has become stretched in defence, an immediate attack can be launched up the centre of the field. If this can be achieved at speed and supported at speed, a try is likely and, if scored, will undoubtedly be a thrilling one. Counter-attack can be very effective because the team that was on attack is likely to be slow in reorganising its defence.

Above: Andrew Mehrtens breaks with good support from All Blacks Alama Ieremia and Jeff Wilson. The options are to form an arrowhead or for both to move to one side if there is space to attack on that side.

Right: Semo Sititi at full speed for Manu Samoa gets around the Scottish defence and is bound for the goal line.

Below right: The attack must continue past the last line of defence all the way to the goal line, as Jonah Lomu demonstrates against Tonga.

Left: Communication is as important on attack as defence. The Sharks' Joggie Viljoen seems to be signalling to his team-mates as he makes a break.

Gareth Edwards was always a dominant figure at Welsh and British Lions practices. At one session it had been decided to introduce a couple of moves involving flankers. When the blind-side flanker was to break, the code would begin with the letter 'P', and when the open-side flanker was involved, the word would begin with 'S'. Coach John Dawes wanted the move practised once more. Edwards put the ball in and shouted 'psychology'. Neither flanker moved.

133

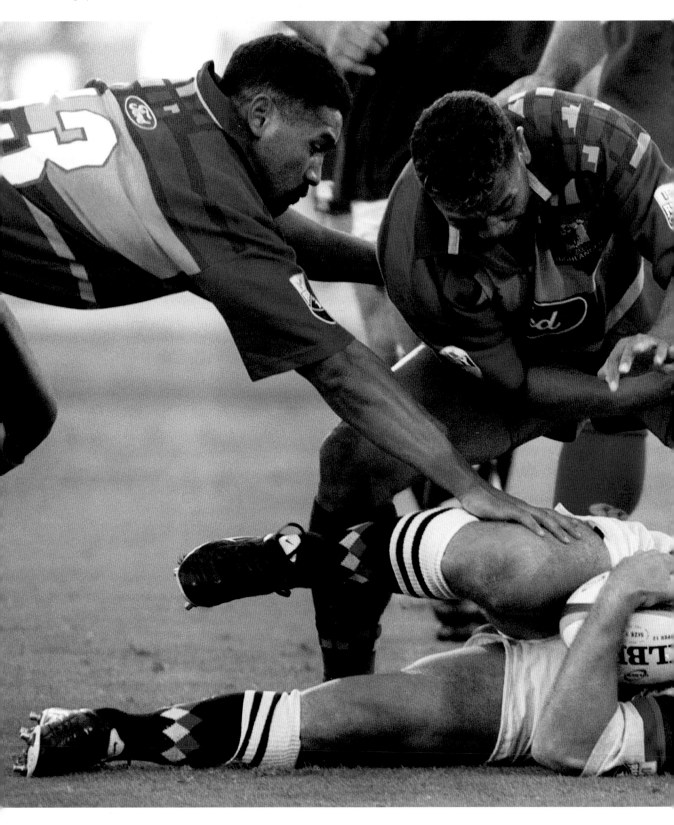

14

Coaching

Team selection

The first rule of team selection is: *Every team is different. Select the player for the plan or the plan for the player.*

When choosing players, decide what ingredients you require. Set down the requirements for each position. Write them down and keep going back to them as you search for or select your players. Exhaust every avenue until you find the players that most closely match your requirements.

Goals

Once the players are identified and notified, they must be part of a long-term goal which the management team, the captain, the vice captains, the players' committee, the senior players and all members of the squad should all know and agree with. There must be no hidden agendas.

The long-term goal is achieved by setting and meeting short-term goals. These goals must be realistic. Even smaller goals can then be set which might be performance-related rather than scoreboard-related. Improved performance leads to improved results.

Keep things basic. Keep things simple. The most effective way is to plan slowly and evolve slowly, so that there is a continuous but gradual improvement throughout the team.

You as coach

- Be yourself. Don't try and be someone else.
- Be honest. Never lie to a player. They will always find you out. Tell it straight.

Craig Innes of the Auckland Blues is on the ground and must release or place the ball. The Otago Highlanders players can pick it up as long as they are on their feet and a ruck has not formed.

- You are the coach, the guide, the manager, but your most important role is not to talk, but to listen, because you are the problem solver.
- Don't try to do it all yourself. Share the problem and use the abilities of the team to help to solve it.
- Don't be too proud. If you don't know how to solve a problem a player is experiencing, find someone who can.

The players

- Create a feeling of self-esteem among the players and strive always to maintain it.
- Stimulate the players into thinking about and discovering their own solutions to problems. Encourage an open mind.
- Ensure each player knows his role. Test them on it. Don't let them be confused.
- Be realistic. It is unreasonable to expect excellence straight away. Don't undermine their confidence by expecting them to be of too high a standard too soon.
- Get them to seek improved performance ahead of seeking results on the scoreboard.

Below: Tries and smiles — they go together.

Above: James Kerr of the Canterbury Crusaders tackles Queensland full-back Nathan Williams while he is jumping for a high ball and so gives away a penalty.

Below: When a coach follows a plan based on the resources of his team, success will follow — John Eales holds the World Cup aloft for Australia (1999).

Training

- Practices should be planned. Write down the tasks on cards. Keep the cards for later reference. Be organised and stick tightly to times and schedules.
- Structure the practice to involve the whole squad. Work on communication and teamwork. Aim for mistake-free activity. Make it enjoyable.
- Tell the players what you want to achieve at the beginning of each training session.
- Share the 'voice load' at practice. Get the players to take on responsibility for some of it.
- Encourage players to communicate constructively about the tasks at hand but allow no idle or destructive chatter.
- Do the accuracy drills early in training as fatigue will reduce thinking ability and skill levels later in the session.

Team pattern

The first thing the coach and his team have to do is decide on the pattern of rugby they wish to play. They have to answer five basic questions:

- How are they going to win possession of the ball?
- How are they going to retain possession of the ball?
- How are they going to use the ball?
- What defensive patterns will the opposition deploy?
- How committed will the defence be?

The coach has to make sure the whole team is involved. He wants every player to contribute 100 per cent. He must also plan strategies and tactics to take advantage of the actual strengths of his team. One player may have exceptional speed. Another may be able to kick long clearing distances with his left foot. The coach must take advantage of these talents in his attacking and defensive plans.

When you join the energy resource of the players to a realistic plan, success will come.

Enjoyment

A team should express itself to the fullest extent of its ability, play to the team plan and have fun. Rugby is an exciting and thrilling game. Learn and practise how to play it properly and enjoy!

15

The Rules
Laws of the Game of Rugby Football

Rugby is a simple game, but the rules can sometimes appear complex and intimidating. With that in mind this abbreviated version has been written in plain English to allow new and younger players to get a grasp of the main laws. It does not cover every possible variation of the laws, so coaches and captains of senior teams are encouraged to become familiar with the official version published by the International Rugby Board and its member unions.

This guide is based on the laws issued by the International Rugby Board as at April 2000. The governing body of a particular country may also modify some of the laws to suit local competitions and age-group competitions.

Object

The object of the game is that two teams of fifteen players score as many points as possible by carrying, passing, kicking and grounding the ball. They should play fairly according to the laws and with a sporting spirit. The team scoring the most points is the winner of the match.

LAW 1 • THE GROUND

The playing area
• The playing area is the field of play and the in-goal area.

The field of play
• Though they define the boundaries of the field of play, the goal lines and the touchlines are considered to be outside it. When the ball touches the touchline it is out of play.

Under the eye of referee Derek Bevan, the Australian No. 8 lifts his head, but makes sure his arms are still bound.

The in-goal area

- The in-goal area is the area behind the goal line which includes the goal line, but does not include the touch-in-goal lines and the dead ball lines.
- When the ball touches the touch-in-goal lines, the dead ball lines, or the corner flag it is considered to be out of play.
- When the ball touches the goal line it is considered to have been touched down in the in-goal area.

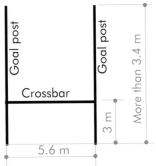

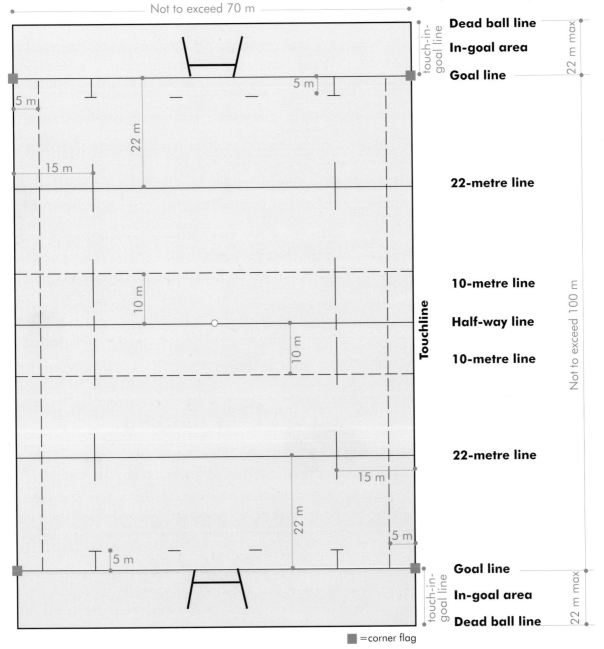

■ = corner flag

Law 2 • THE BALL

- The ball should be oval and about 280 to 300 mm long. At its widest point it should have a circumference of 580 to 620 mm and should weigh between 400 to 440 grams. These sizes can be reduced for age-group rugby.

Law 3 • THE NUMBER OF PLAYERS AND THE REPLACEMENT OF PLAYERS

- A team can consist of no more than fifteen players on the playing area during a match. Matches can be played with fewer than fifteen players, but there cannot be fewer than three players per team in a scrum.
- Only front row forwards can play in the front row of the scrum. If there are not enough front row forwards because of injuries in the match, the scrums must be carried out without pushing and the team putting the ball in must win it.
- For international matches a team can have up to seven replacement players on the bench.
- If a player has a bleeding or open wound he must leave the field to have it bandaged (blood bin). Another player from his team can take his place on the field until he returns. However, an injured player who has been permanently replaced cannot take any further part in the match.
- Players can only be replaced when the ball is dead and with the permission of the referee.

Law 4 • PLAYERS' DRESS

- The players may wear jerseys, shorts and undergarments, socks and boots (known as rugby shoes in the United States). They can also wear shin guards, mitts (fingerless gloves) and shoulder pads made of soft, thin materials. Women may wear chest pads of soft, thin materials. Players can also wear mouthguards and headgear made of soft and thin materials, thin tape, bandages and dressings to cover or protect an injury.
- Anything hard, such as zips and jewellery, should not be worn.
- Studs (cleats) on boots must not be longer than 18 mm.

Law 5 • TOSS, TIME

- Before a match begins the captains toss a coin. The one who calls correctly gets to choose whether to kick-off or which end to defend.
- The match is 80 minutes long, but more time can be played for a knockout competition. Time is also added on when play has been stopped to attend to injured players (extra time).
- Play is divided into two halves with a half-time break of no more than ten minutes. At halftime the teams change ends.

Law 6 • REFEREE AND TOUCH JUDGES

- Every match played must have a referee. If one has not been appointed, it is the home team's responsibility to appoint one. During a match the referee should not consult with anyone except the touch judges. The referee's decision is final.
- The referee must carry a whistle and must blow it every time he has to stop play for any reason.
- There are two touch judges for every match. Unless the touch judges have been appointed by the host union, it is the responsibility of each team to provide one touch judge for the match, each of whom is under the control of the referee.
- The touch judge carries a flag or other suitable object, which he holds up when the player carrying the ball has gone into touch, or when the ball goes into touch. He holds the flag in the air and with his other arm points in the direction of the team which gets the throw in.

Law 7 • MODE OF PLAY

- A match is started by a kick-off from the centre of the field of play.

Law 8 • ADVANTAGE

- When a team commits an infringement which results in a clear advantage to the other team then the referee allows play to go on. The referee is the sole judge of whether an advantage has been gained.

Law 9 • BALL OR PLAYER TOUCHING THE REFEREE

- If the ball or player touches the referee in the field of play, the play continues unless the referee considers that one side has gained an advantage from this. If the referee feels an advantage has been gained, he orders a scrum and the team that had possession of the ball gets the put-in.
- If the referee is similarly touched in the in-goal area, then unless he considers an unfair advantage has been gained he awards a try (if the ball carrier is from the attacking team) or a five-metre scrum with the put-in to the attacking team (if the ball carrier is from the defending team).
- If the ball touches the referee, a touch judge or a spectator in the in-goal area and is not held by a player, the referee awards a try if it is believed that a try would have been scored.

Law 10 • THE KICK-OFF

- The kick-off is taken from the middle of the half-way line at the beginning of the match, and at the restart after the break. Each team gets one kick-off per match.
- A kick-off also restarts the match after one team has scored. The team that has not scored takes the kick-off, which must be a drop kick.
- At the kick-off, the ball must cross the opponents' ten-metre line, even if it is blown back by the wind. If the ball fails to cross the line, the defending team has the choice of having the kick taken again or a scrum at the point the kick was taken.
- If from a kick-off, the ball crosses the opposing team's goal line, they can ground the ball and then have the choice of making the other team kick-off again or having a scrum in the centre of the field.
- The kicker's team must be behind the ball when he kicks it or a scrum will be formed in the middle of the field with the put-in to the other team.
- The opposing team must stand on or behind the ten-metre line. If they are in front of the ten-metre line or charge before the ball has been kicked, then the kick has to be retaken.

Law 11 • METHOD OF SCORING

- **Try** (5 points): A try is scored by a player grounding the ball in the opponent's in-goal area.
- **Goal** (3 points): A goal is scored by kicking the ball over the opponent's crossbar and between the goalposts, using a place kick or a drop kick from a position in the field of play. A drop goal cannot be directly scored from a kick-off, a 22-metre drop-out or from a free kick.
- **Conversion** (2 points): A conversion is a kick at goal awarded immediately after a try from a position in the field of play in line with the point at which the try was scored.
- **Penalty try** (5 points plus 2 more if converted): A penalty try is awarded by the referee if a try would probably have been scored but for foul play by the defending team preventing it from being scored. The conversion is in line from the middle of the goalposts.

Law 12 • TRY AND TOUCHDOWN

The ball is grounded by a player:
- when he holds the ball in his hands or arms and brings it into contact with the ground, or
- when the ball is on the ground and he places a hand or an arm on it with downward pressure, or
- when he falls on the ball anywhere under the front of his body, from the waist up.
- A try is also scored if a player is tackled outside the in-goal area but his momentum carries him forward over the goal line and he then grounds the ball.

- **Touchdown:** A touchdown is when the *defending* team touches the ball down in their own in-goal area. The ball can be touched down in exactly the same way that a try can be scored.
- If the defending team has brought the ball back over their own goal line, then play is restarted with a five-metre scrum, and the put-in goes to the attacking team.
- If the ball has been taken over the goal line by the attacking team and touched down by the defending team, then play is restarted with a drop kick by the defending team, from behind their own 22-metre line.

Law 13 • KICK AT GOAL AFTER A TRY

- After a try has been scored, the successful team has a right to take a kick at goal (either a place kick or a drop kick) from a position in the field of play in line with the point at which the try was scored. The rest of the team must stand behind the kicker, except for one team member who is allowed to steady the ball, if needed. The kicker can use sand, sawdust or an approved kicking tee to place the ball.
- When the kick is being taken the opposing team must stand behind the goal line. They are not allowed to distract the kicker. When the kicker starts his approach, they are allowed to run at him in an attempt to charge down the kick.

Law 14 • IN-GOAL

- In the in-goal area, the ball is said to be in touch (out of play) when it or the person holding it touches the corner post (not the flag) or a touch-in-goal line, or the dead ball line.
- When the ball or the player carrying it touches the ground within these lines (including the goal line itself) or the goal post, the ball is said to be grounded.
- The ball also becomes 'dead' when knocked over the in-goal touchlines or dead ball line.

Law 15 • DROP-OUT

- A drop-out is a drop kick awarded to the defending team. The drop kick can be taken from anywhere behind the defending team's 22-metre line and must cross the 22-metre line (even if blown back by the wind).
- The kicker's team must be behind the ball when the drop kick is taken. If they are in front of the kicker they are deemed offside and a scrum is awarded to the attacking team. However, the kick can be taken quickly, even if players of the defending team are in front of the kicker, only when those players are retreating to an onside position and they take no part in the play.
- If the drop-out is kicked directly into touch the opposing team has the choice of accepting the lineout, having the drop-out re-taken, or having a scrum at the centre of the 22-metre line.

Law 16 • FAIR CATCH OR MARK

- A player can make a fair catch (a mark) in his own 22-metre area or in his own in-goal area when he catches the ball directly from a kick by the opposition team (even if it touches the posts or crossbar). But he cannot make a mark from the opposition kick-off or if the ball has touched one of his own players in flight.
- If he wishes to claim the mark when catching the ball he must shout, 'mark'. The referee will then award him a free kick. Only the player who made the mark can take it and he must do it from the exact point that he caught the ball. He can, however, kick the ball a short distance into the air, catch it himself and pass it to a specialist kicker who, because he is behind his 22-metre line, can kick the ball directly to touch.

Law 17 • KNOCK-ON OR THROW FORWARD

- A knock-on is when the ball is propelled by a hand or arm in the direction of the opponent's dead ball line.
- If a player juggles the ball while in possession of it and regains it before it hits the ground, it is not a knock-on.
- If a kick is charged down by a player who is not attempting to catch the ball it is not a knock-on.
- A throw forward (forward pass) is when the ball is thrown or passed in the direction of the opponent's dead ball line.
- If a knock-on or throw forward is accidental, a scrum is awarded against the offending team.
- If the referee considers a knock-on or a throw forward to be deliberate, he can award a penalty or a penalty try against the offending team.
- The referee can also play advantage when there is a knock-on or a throw forward.

Law 18 • TACKLE, LYING WITH, ON OR NEAR THE BALL

- A player with the ball is said to be tackled when he is held, sitting or lying on the ground or has at least one knee on the ground.
- A tackled player must immediately pass or release the ball and move away from it. He is allowed to place the ball in a backward

direction with his hand. He is allowed to place it forward only if attempting to score a try.

- The tackler must release the tackled player and also move away from the ball. He cannot play it again until he is on his feet. No player can play the ball after a tackle unless he is on his feet. However, if the ball is in the in-goal area, any player who is not on his feet is allowed to fall on it in order to ground it.
- Players not involved in the tackle can only enter the tackled ball area from their team's side of the ball and from behind the last player in the tackle.
- If a player involved in the tackle fails to move away from a tackled ball situation or interferes with the release of the ball in any way, the referee should award a penalty against him.

LAW 19 • TACKLE, LYING WITH, ON OR NEAR THE BALL

This law has now been included in Law 18.

LAW 20 • SCRUMMAGE

- The scrum takes place at the point of the infringement, but no closer than five metres to the touchline. For safety reasons, each front row should follow the referee's instructions to 'crouch, pause (or wait) and engage'. The referee does not call the front rows to engage until the ball is in the hands of the player putting it in.
- There are eight players from each team in a scrum, all of whom have to remain bound until the scrum ends. The front row must always have three players from each side and their weight should be placed firmly on at least one foot.
- When a scrum collapses the referee must whistle immediately to stop the players pushing and to stop play. No front row player must do anything likely to cause the scrum to collapse. When a scrum collapses, the team that has the put-in retains it.
- If any player in the scrum is lifted off his feet the referee will stop play and reset the scrum.
- If a scrum wheels through 90 degrees or the referee deems it stationary for too long with no sign of the ball coming out, the scrum is reset with the put-in going to the other team.

- The scrum is at an end when the ball is in the scrum over the goal line or when the ball comes out of the scrum or when the hindmost player in the scrum, the No. 8, disengages to pick up the ball at his feet.

Binding of players

All players must remain bound until the scrum has ended. Specifically:

- The loosehead prop must bind with his left arm inside the right arm of his opponent or place his left hand or forearm on his own left thigh. He can alter his binding during the scrum.
- The tighthead prop must bind with his right arm outside the left upper arm of the opposing loosehead prop. He must grip the jersey, but not the arm or the sleeve, of the opposing loosehead prop with his right hand. He is not allowed to exert a downward pressure.
- Any player in the scrum who is not a front row player must bind with one arm around a lock.
- No player is allowed to handle the ball in the scrum.

Putting the ball into the scrum

- The ball should be put into the scrum as soon as the two front rows have engaged. The player putting the ball in stands one metre from the tunnel of the scrum. He holds the ball in two hands and puts it into the tunnel in a single movement so that it touches the ground immediately past the nearest prop. If the ball comes straight out of the tunnel, it is put in again.
- The player who puts the ball into the scrum and his immediate opposite (usually the two scrum-halves) should not try to trick their opponents into believing the ball is out of the scrum.

Law 21 • RUCK

- A ruck is formed *when the ball is on the ground* and one or more opposing players are on their feet and in physical contact above it. A player joining a ruck must bind with at least one arm around the body of a player of his team in the ruck.
- Players must not kick the ball back into the ruck or do anything to trick the opposition into believing the ball is out of the ruck. They cannot handle the ball in the ruck except while scoring a try or a touchdown. Players should not lie on the ground in such

a way as to prevent the ball coming out of a ruck.

- Standing players should only ruck the ball, not the man.
- When the ball becomes trapped in a ruck the referee will blow for a scrum. The put-in goes to the team that was last moving forward before the referee blew his whistle. If no team was moving forward the put-in goes to the attacking team.

Law 22 • MAUL

- A maul is formed *when the ball is off the ground* by one or more opposing players on their feet and in physical contact with a player in possession of the ball.
- Players are not allowed to collapse a maul, jump on top of players in a maul or drag a player out of a maul or trick the opponents into believing the ball has come out of the maul.
- If a maul becomes stationary or the ball is unplayable or the person holding the ball has at least one knee on the ground, the referee orders a scrum. The put-in goes to the team who did not have possession of the ball when the maul started (use it or lose it). If the referee is unable to decide which team had the ball, the put-in is awarded to the team that was going forward. If neither team was going forward, the put-in is awarded to the attacking team. However, if a maul occurs as a result of a catch following a kick by an opponent (other than a kick-off or free kick), the catcher's team gets the put-in if the maul becomes stationary.

Law 23 • TOUCH AND LINEOUT

Touch

- The ball is in touch (off the field of play) when it crosses or touches a touchline or when a player carrying the ball touches the line or the ground beyond it.
- A player who is off the field may touch the ball with his hand as long as he does not hold it and as long as the ball has not yet crossed the touchline.
- The ball is kicked 'directly' into touch if it is kicked from outside the kicker's 22 and it does not bounce before it crosses the touchline.
- If the ball goes into touch directly from a kick-off, the opposing team has the option of calling a lineout on the half-way line or

where the ball went into touch if that is nearer the kicker's goal line.

- If the ball goes into touch directly from a drop-out the opposing team has the choice of accepting the lineout where the ball went into touch, having the drop-out retaken, or having a scrum at the centre of the 22-metre line.

Lineout

- Lineouts are formed at right angles to the touchline by at least two players from each team who must stand one metre from their opponents. The lineout begins five metres from the touchline and ends 15 metres from the touchline.
- A lineout can take place no closer than one metre to the goal line.
- The team throwing the ball in decides how many players will be in the lineout but they do not have to tell the other team. If there are more players in the lineout on the opposing side, the extra players should withdraw from the lineout and retire ten metres.
- The scrum-half and the non-throwing hooker can take part in jumping for the ball at the lineout.

Throwing in the ball

- The ball is thrown into the lineout from the point at which it crossed the touchline. However, when the ball has been kicked directly into touch from outside the kicker's 22-metre area ('out on the full'), the throw is taken from a line level with the point where the kick was made. The player throwing the ball in must not put either foot into the field of play.
- When the ball is kicked into touch from a penalty kick, the kicker's team gets to throw the ball into the lineout.
- The ball must be thrown straight between the two opposing lines and go at least five metres. If the throw is not straight the opposing team gets the option of taking the throw itself or having the put-in to a scrum 15 metres infield.
- A quick throw-in can be taken at any point between where the ball crossed the touchline and the throwing-in team's own goal line, but it must be taken before a proper lineout has formed. The throw must be taken from behind the touchline with the same ball that went out by the same player who retrieved it — he must be the only player to have touched the ball.
- When there is doubt about which team last touched the ball

before it went into touch, the throw-in is given to the attacking team.

Beginning and end of a lineout

- The lineout begins when it leaves the hands of the thrower. No player can support another or jump for the ball until it has left the hands of the thrower. The lineout ends when one of the following occurs:
  - the ball has left the lineout,
  - the lineout (or a ruck or maul formed from it) has moved from the line of the lineout, or
  - the ball becomes unplayable.

Peeling off

- Peeling off is when a player leaves the lineout to catch the ball being thrown down to him by a jumper at the lineout. Until the lineout ends, the only player allowed to leave it is the one peeling off.

Restrictions on players in the lineout

- Players must not hold, push, grab or use an opponent for support.
- A player must jump for the ball with both hands or the inside arm only.
- Support players must not assist a jumper from below the waist.

Law 24 • OFFSIDE

There are many definitions of offside but generally it means a player is in a position where he gains an unfair advantage.

A. Offside in general play

- A player is offside if he is in front of the ball after it has been played by one of his team-mates. However he will not be penalised if:
  - he makes no attempt to play the ball,
  - he has retired ten metres from where the ball lands, or
  - he waits for the kicker or his team-mates to come up and put him onside.
- When the offside player cannot help being touched by the ball or the player holding the ball, he is considered to be accidentally offside. He is not penalised unless an advantage is obtained for

his team, at which point the referee awards a scrum with the put-in given to the opposing team.
- When a member of a team is offside, the referee can play advantage for the opposing team, but if no advantage results he awards a penalty to the opposing team.

B. Offside at the scrum
- If he is not involved in the scrum or putting the ball into the scrum, a player must remain behind the hindmost feet of the scrum or behind the goal line if that is nearer.
- The scrum-half whose team has possession of the ball in the scrum must keep at least one foot level with or behind the ball while it is in the scrum.
- The opposing scrum-half must keep both feet behind the ball while it is in the scrum.

C. Offside at ruck or maul
- A player must join a ruck or maul from behind the hindmost player of his team in the ruck or maul. He must not join from his opponent's side. If a player disengages from the ruck or maul, he must retire past the hindmost feet.

D. Offside at a lineout
- For a player involved in a lineout to remain onside during the lineout, he must not:
    - cross the centre line of the lineout,
    - move in front of the ball,
    - be more than 15 metres from the touchline (except for a long throw-in by his own team, in which case the player cannot leave the lineout until the ball leaves the thrower's hands).
- Players not involved directly in the lineout must not advance beyond the offside line (ten metres from the hindmost feet of the lineout) until the lineout is over. They may come forward for a long throw-in, but only after the ball has left the hands of the thrower.

Law 25 • ONSIDE

Onside means that a player is in the game and not offside.
- When a player has been offside, he can be made onside by himself or his own team by:

- going back behind the player on his side who last touched the ball,
- one of his team who has the ball running in front of him,
- one of his team running past him who has come from where the ball was kicked,
- going back ten metres from where the ball lands or is caught by the opposition. However, a player who is offside because he is within ten metres of where the ball is going to land cannot be put onside by his opponents.
- An offside player can be brought onside by the opposition by:
  - an opponent running more than five metres with the ball,
  - an opponent kicking or passing the ball,
  - an opponent touching the ball intentionally, but not picking it up or catching it.
- In general play, any offside player is put onside when his opponent plays the ball.

Players offside at a scrum, ruck or lineout who are returning to their own side
- Such a player becomes onside when:
  - an opponent with the ball has run five metres, or
  - an opponent has kicked the ball.
- He is not put onside when an opponent passes the ball.
- Players who are standing in an offside position should not prevent the opposition from passing, running or kicking.

Law 26 • FOUL PLAY

Foul play is any type of play or behaviour which breaks the rules or is against the spirit of rugby. It includes obstruction, unfair play, misconduct, dangerous play, unsporting behaviour, retaliation and repeated infringements.

Obstruction
All the following are illegal:
- Charging or pushing an opponent when both are running for the ball (shoulder to shoulder contact is acceptable).
- A player who by being offside, stops an opponent from tackling one of his own players who has the ball.
- A player who has the ball running through his own team at a scrum, lineout, ruck or maul.

- A player who is bound on the outside of the scrum, stopping an opponent coming around the scrum.

Unfair play, repeated infringements

It is illegal for a player to:
- Break any law of the game.
- Deliberately keep breaking a law.
- Deliberately knock or throw the ball from the field of play.
- Deliberately waste time.

Misconduct, dangerous play

It is illegal for a player to:
- Strike an opponent.
- To kick, trip or trample an opponent.
- To tackle an opponent early or late or to tackle him with a stiff arm. No tackling is allowed above the line of the shoulders.
- To charge or obstruct an opponent who has just kicked the ball.
- To hold, grab, push, charge or obstruct an opponent who does not have the ball (except in a scrum, ruck or maul).
- Charge or knock down an opponent who is carrying the ball, but without making any attempt to tackle him.
- Tap or pull the feet of a player jumping in a lineout.
- Tackle a player when he is in the air while jumping for a ball.
- To play in any way contrary to the spirit of good conduct or sportsmanship.

Misconduct, dangerous play in a scrum

It is illegal for a player to:
- Charge at the opposing front row in a scrum from a distance.
- Lift a player in the opposing front row up or off his feet.
- Cause a scrum, ruck or maul to collapse.

It *is* permitted to drag away an opponent lying close to the ball in open play.

Both the following are illegal because of the potential danger:

Flying wedge: to charge at the opposition in a wedge or V formation with one player near the front carrying the ball.
Cavalry charge: to charge at the opposition in a long line when taking the ball from a tap kick.

The consequences

- When a player is guilty of misconduct he will be warned. When he is repeatedly guilty of misconduct or his offence is serious, he will be ordered off to take no further part in the match. A report will be sent to the Union or other disciplinary body. The player has the right to submit evidence in his defence. If the disciplinary body finds the player guilty, it may decide to impose further punishment.
- When a player has been guilty of foul play that has not been seen by the match officials, he can be cited after the match by officials of either team participating in the match or officials of the Unions if it is an international match.
- When a front row player is sent off, he can be replaced by another front row player of his team, but one of his team-mates has to leave the field.
- When different players of a team are guilty of repeatedly committing the same offence the referee should warn the whole team and then send off the next player of that team to commit the offence. This can be varied for age-group rugby where players are not so aware of the laws.
- A player guilty of dangerous play or misconduct can also be ordered off the field for a short period (the sin bin). He must remain off the field for the period stipulated by the referee.

PENALTIES

Penalty try

- A penalty try is awarded when a player uses foul play to prevent what would probably have been a try.

Penalty kick

- The non-offending team can decide to take a penalty kick from where the infringement took place or where the ball landed (when kicked). This cannot be closer than five metres from the opponent's goal line.
- If the offending team prevents the non-offending team from taking a penalty once it has been awarded, the referee can move the placement of the penalty ten metres closer to the offending team's line.

LAW 27 • PENALTY KICK

- A penalty kick is a kick awarded to the non-offending team. The non-offending team also has the option of taking a scrum at the point of the offence.

Taking a penalty kick

- A penalty kick can be taken by any player in the team by any method, but he must kick it with his foot or lower leg — he cannot bounce it off his knee. He can use sand, sawdust or an approved kicking tee to place the ball. The kicker must do the following:
  - The kick must be taken without undue delay.
  - The kick must be taken from the mark or behind it.
  - The kicker may kick the ball in any direction, but if he says he is going to kick the ball at goal, he must kick it in that direction.
  - If he is kicking for touch, he can only punt or drop kick the ball.
  - The kicker's team, except for one player — the placer — who can hold the ball steady (if and when necessary) for a place kick, must be behind the ball.

Taking the kick quickly

- If the kick is taken quickly, the referee should not penalise players from the kicker's team who are returning to an onside position. However, these players cannot take any part in the game until they *are* onside. Also:
  - The opposing team must retire ten metres from the mark of the penalty or to their own goal line if it closer than ten metres to the mark.
  - If the kick is taken quickly the opposing players cannot re-enter the game until they have retired ten metres or one of their players who was ten metres from the mark has run in front of them.
  - If the kicker is kicking at goal, the defending team cannot move from their position or attempt to distract the kicker until the ball has been kicked.
  - The penalised team must not delay the kick by throwing or kicking the ball away or interfering with the kicker.

Law 28 • FREE KICK

- A free kick is awarded by the referee for minor offences or for a fair catch. The team awarded the free kick can decide to take a scrum instead. If they take a kick they must do so without delay using the foot or lower leg. They must take the kick from or behind the mark, but no closer than five metres from the opponent's goal line. Also:
    - The kicker can kick the ball any way, but can only punt or drop kick the ball into touch.
    - The kicker's team, except for one player — the placer — who can hold the ball steady (if and when necessary) for a place kick, must be behind the ball.
    - If the kick is taken quickly, the referee should not penalise players from the kicker's team who are returning to an onside position. However, these players cannot take any part in the game until they *are* onside.
    - If the defending team charges the kick fairly and players are able to prevent it being taken, the kick is void. There will then be a scrum at the mark and the opposing team will get the put-in.
    - Neither the kicker nor his team are allowed to cause the opposing team to charge the kick early; if they do, the charge will be allowed.
- A drop goal cannot be scored by the team awarded a free kick until one of the following has occurred:
    - The ball has gone dead.
    - It has been touched by an opposing player.
    - An opposing player has tackled one of the kicker's team.
    - A maul has been formed.

This rule also applies if the attacking team has taken a scrum instead of a free kick.

Glossary

22-metre drop-out – a drop kick to restart play taken by the defending team from behind their 22-metre line.

22-metre line – the line on the field of play that marks a team's defensive zone (also called the 22).

Advantage – when the referee allows play to continue because the non-offending team has possession of the ball and a clear advantage has been gained.

Against the head – winning the ball at the scrum when the other team has put it in.

All Blacks – the New Zealand rugby team.

American football pass – a long one-handed overhead pass across the field (similar to a quarterback pass in American football).

Ankle tap – striking the ball carrier's ankle from behind causing him to lose balance.

'Anything goes' pass – any pass, no matter how awkward, which reaches the receiver.

Backs – the players who stand behind the scrum.

Back three – the fullback and the two wings.

Back row – the three outside (loose) players in the scrum.

Ball carrier – the person carrying the ball.

Binding – holding on to another player with the full use of the arm.

Blind side – the space between the ball and the nearest touchline (compare open side).

Blind-side charge – an attacking move on the blind side of the field.

Blind-side defence – defence on the blind side of the field.

Bobbing ball – the ball bouncing along the ground unevenly.

Body position – the alignment of the whole body when carrying out a technique.

Box kick – a high kick aimed at landing in front of the opposing wing.

Breakdown – when possession of the ball has been temporarily halted and possession is being contested by both sides. A tackle is usually the point of breakdown.

Bump – the ball carrier knocks back the tackler by bumping his shoulder against the tackler's shoulder.

Centre – a playing position in the middle of the backline.

Change-of-direction pass – pretending to pass in one direction, then passing the opposite way.

Channel – a route that the ball takes between the players' legs when coming back through the scrum (there are three main channels).

Chip kick – a short kick over an opponent's head.

Code – secret signals or messages a team uses to communicate planned moves.

Conversion – the kick at goal following a try.

Corner flag – the flags at the corners of the goal line and the touchline.

Counter-attack – an attacking move in response to an opposition attack after possession has changed hands.

Cross kick – a kick across the field towards the attacking team's open wing position.

Cut-back pass – *see* Scissors

Cut-out pass – a pass that misses out a player

in the attacking team and is intended for the next player out (also called a miss-pass).

Dart – a sudden movement in a different direction.

Dead ball line – the line at each end of the field of play. When the ball or the player carrying the ball touches it, the ball is said to be 'dead'.

Decoy – a player who pretends he is about to get the ball to confuse the opposition.

Defence – the system, tactics or actions used to counter an opposition attack.

Defensive scrum – a scrum in which the opposition puts in the ball.

Delaying the pass – the ball carrier holding on to the ball longer than usual before passing to try to break up the rhythm of the defence.

Distractor – a player who pretends he is going to be part of an attack when he isn't.

Dive pass – passing the ball while diving towards the catcher.

Dodge – to move quickly to the side to avoid a tackler.

Drawing the man – committing an opponent to making the tackle before passing.

Drift defence – a system of defence that drifts sideways across the field.

Drive – to push forward by driving the legs hard against the ground.

Driving maul – a maul in which the opposition is driven back.

Driving tackle – when the tackler pushes the ball carrier backwards.

Drop goal – a drop kick from the field of play which sends the ball over the crossbar.

Drop kick – a kick which strikes the ball immediately after it has been deliberately dropped to the ground.

Drop-out – a restart of play in which the defending team drop kicks from behind their own 22-metre line.

Drubber kick – a low bouncing kick across the ground (same as grubber kick)

Dummy or **dummy pass** – a pretended pass.

Dummy kick – a pretended kick.

Engagement – when the opposing front rows of the scrum come together.

Extra time – time added on by the referee for injuries and stoppages.

Fair catch – a player catching the ball inside his own 22 when the opposition has kicked it (also called a mark).

Fast pass – when the ball is passed as soon as it is caught because the receiver is about to be tackled.

Feint – a faked move to deceive an opponent.

Fend – when the ball carrier uses the arm and open hand to push off an opponent (also called a hand-off).

Field of play – the whole of the playing field between the two dead ball lines.

First five-eighths – the fly-half.

Five-metre scrum – a scrum five metres from the defending team's goal line; see Law 20.

Flanker – one of the two players on either side, or flank, of the scrum.

Flick pass – a pass using a flick of the wrists.

Fly-half – the back who stands between the scrum-half and the inside centre.

Forward charge – an aggressive run by a forward with the ball, trying to knock his opponents out of the way.

Forward pass – when a player throws a pass ahead of himself. This is an illegal move in rugby.

Foul play – play that is dangerous or against the rules or the spirit of the game.

Free kick – a lesser grade of penalty which, when awarded, does not allow the kicker to take a direct kick at goal.

Front-on tackle – a tackle in which the ball carrier runs straight at the tackler.

Front row – the first row of forwards in the scrum, consisting of two props and a hooker.

Fullback – the player nearest his own goal posts.

Full stop – to suddenly stop dead with the ball, confusing the opposition.

Full time – the end of the match.

Gain line – an imaginary line between the two teams that must be crossed for one team to gain a territorial advantage over the other.

Gang tackle – two or more opposing players tackling the ball carrier.

Garryowen – the up-and-under kick, named after an Irish club that used it frequently.

Goal – a successful kick between the goal posts.

Goal line – the try line.

Goal posts – the upright posts that make up the goal.

Goose step – a short step with the knees locked.

Grounding – forcing the ball against the ground in the in-goal area with the hands, arms or upper body.

Grubber – a short, flat kick (also called a drubber kick).

Gumshield – a plastic guard that is placed in the mouth over the upper row of teeth (a mouthguard).

Hack kick – a kick ahead of the loose ball.

Halfback – the back closest to the scrum.

Halfback pass – a long pass from the forwards to the backs.

Half hold – when the ball carrier is held but not fully tackled.

Hand-off – when the ball carrier uses the arm and open hand to push off an opponent (also called a fend).

High tackle – a dangerous and illegal tackle above the line of the shoulders.

Hit and spin – a forward charge in which the ball carrier manages to spin out of the tackle.

Hooker – the player who hooks back the ball in the scrum.

Hospital pass – a poorly timed pass which reaches the catcher at the same time as the tackler (and risks injury).

In-goal – the area of the field between the goal posts and the dead ball line.

Infringement – breaking one of the rules for which the referee will award a penalty to the non-offending team.

Inside centre – centre closest to the scrum.

In touch – off the field of play.

Jump – to leap vertically off the ground, usually to catch the ball.

Kick-off – the start of a match or the restart after one team has scored.

Knock-on – when the ball has struck a player's hands or arms, gone forward and hit the ground or another player.

Line – 1. The line of the backs or forwards of one team; 2. the goal line; 3. any line marked on the field.

Lineout – the players lined up to catch the ball when it is thrown back onto the field.

Lob pass – a pass over an opponent's head.

Lock – one of the two second row forwards in the middle of the scrum.

Long pass – a longer than normal pass across the field.

Loop – running around a team-mate that a player has just passed to in order to receive the ball back from him again.

Loosehead prop – the prop on the left side of his own scrum.

Loosie – a common name for the three players of the back row of the scrum who are able to disengage more quickly than the tight five. They are the players expected to be first to the loose ball or breakdown.

Man-on-man defence – a system of defence in which the tackler takes the man directly opposite him.

Man-out defence – a system of defence in which the tacklers line up their men from the outside of the field inwards.

Mark – 1. The place a penalty, free kick or scrum is taken from; 2. a defender catching the ball from an opposition kick inside his own 22 (also called a fair catch).

Marking – watching and staying with an opponent, ready to tackle him.

Maul – a wrestle for the ball between both teams.

Miss-out pass – a pass which misses out one attacking player and is meant for the next player in the line (also called a cut-out pass).

Mobile – being able to move rapidly around the field.

Mouthguard – a plastic guard that is placed in the mouth over the upper row of teeth.

No. 8 – the player at the back of the scrum.

Non-offending team – the team that has not broken the law (compare offending).

Non-pass – when the ball carrier changes his running action as if about to pass, but doesn't and speeds up again.

Normal pass – the normal pass made by a running player using a swing of the arms and body to pass the ball to a team-mate.

Obstruction – illegally getting in the way of an opposition player.

Offending team – the team that has broken the law (compare non-offending).

Offside – when a player is standing where he is not allowed to, usually in front of the ball. See Law 24 for more information.

One-handed pass – passing the ball with one hand.

One-handed tap back – a lineout jumper knocking the ball back towards his own side with one hand.

Onside – being in a fair position, usually behind the ball.

Open play – when play is moving about the field without being stopped by the referee.

Open rugby – fast, flowing rugby.

Open side – the space between the ball and the farthest touchline (compare blind side).

Out – off the field of play.

Outside centre – the centre who stands furthermost from his own scrum.

Outside cut – a swerve towards the outside of the field.

Overhead pass – when a player lifts the ball above his head to get the pass over the head of a tackler.

Over-the-shoulder kick – a kick, often made by the scrum-half, when facing the wrong way and under pressure from the opposition.

Over-the-top throw – a long throw which goes right over the top of the lineout.

Overlap – when one side has an extra player on the outside.

Pass – a player throwing the ball to a team-mate.

Passing on – when the ball is quickly passed out towards the wings.

Peel – a move in which a forward runs the ball up from the lineout.

Penalty – a free kick awarded to one team when the other team has broken the rules.

Penalty kick – a free kick of the ball given to the non-offending team because the opposition has broken a rule.

Penalty try – a try awarded by the referee when the attacking team would have scored but for foul play by the opposition.

Penetrator – an attacking player who breaks through the defence of the opposition.

Pick-and-go – a forward charge in which the ball is put on the ground in the tackle and the next forward picks it up and runs with it.

Pivot – a player who sets up a penetration move.

Place kick – kicking the ball after it is placed on the ground.

Pop pass – a very short pass.

Positions – where the players stand on the field, which is fixed in set play.

Prop – the players in the scrum who support the hooker.

Punt – to kick the ball from the hand.

Pushover try – a try scored as a result of the attacking team pushing their opponent's scrum over their own goal line.

Quality ball – good, clean possession that can be used to create an attack.

Quick throw-in – a throw into the lineout taken quickly before the lineout has formed.

Referee – the official on the field who ensures both teams keep to the laws of the game.

Retire – to resume an onside position, either: 1. behind a team-mate about to kick the ball, or 2. ten metres distant from an opposing player about to take a free kick or penalty.

Reverse flick – a pass thrown backwards by the ball carrier to a team-mate behind him.

Reverse pass – a pass out of the back of the hand.

Ripping the ball – pulling the ball free at a maul (also called stripping the ball).

Rolling maul – a maul in which the attacking team constantly changes the point of attack to the left or the right while going forward.

Ruck – when the ball is on the ground and both teams are trying to push each other off it.

Rules – the agreed laws on how the game will be played.

Scissors – passing to a player who cuts back in the opposite direction (also known as a cut-back pass).

Screw kick – a kick which causes the ball to spin through the air (also called spiral kick).

Scrum – a set-piece pushing contest between two teams.

Scrum-half – the halfback.

Scrum-half pass – a long pass by the scrum-half to clear the ball from his forwards to his backs.

Scrum machine – a machine used at scrum practice.

Scrummage – a scrum.

Second five-eighths – the inside centre.

Second phase – when both teams are contesting possession of the ball.

Second row – the two locks, the second row of forwards in the scrum.

Set piece – a set way of restarting play such as a scrum or lineout (same as set play).

Set play – a set way of restarting play such as a scrum or lineout (same as set piece).

Shortened lineout – when the team throwing in calls for fewer than seven players to take part in the lineout.

Side-on tackle – a tackle made into the side of the ball carrier.

Side-step – to evade a tackler by quickly stepping to one side before proceeding.

Smother tackle – a type of tackle in which the ball carrier's arms are held or smothered so that he can't pass the ball.

Spin – the rotation of the ball as it is propelled through the air.

Spiral kick – a kick which causes the ball to spin through the air (also called a screw kick).

Spiral pass – a pass which causes the ball to spin through the air (also called a spin pass).

Stationary tackle – a tackle made when the tackler is standing still and the ball carrier is running at him.

Stiff-arm tackle – a dangerous tackle made with the arm straight.

Stripping the ball – pulling the ball free at a maul (also called ripping the ball).

Swerve – to deviate from a straight line, usually at speed.

Support – to follow closely; to back up the ball carrier.

Tackle – to stop the ball carrier and (usually) take him to the ground.

Tackled ball pass – a pass made by the ball carrier after he has been tackled but still has one or both hands free.

Tactics – way of working as a team to beat the opposition.

Tap kick – a short penalty kick used when the attacking team intends to run with the ball.

Tap penalty – same as tap kick.

Team – a group of players who are all on the same side.

Technique – the exact means of achieving one's purpose.

Ten-metre line – the line either side of the half-way line past which the ball has to be kicked at a kick-off.

Threequarters – the centres and wings.

Throw-forward – when the ball is thrown, deliberately or accidentally, in the direction of the opposition goal line (not level or backwards). This is illegal and results in a penalty.

Tight five – the name given to the tightly bound front and second row forwards who are supposed to do the hard or tight work in the scrums, lineouts, rucks and mauls.

Tight head – hooking the ball in the scrum when the other team has put it in.

Tighthead prop – the prop on the right side of his own scrum, furthest away from where his scrum-half puts the ball in.

Touch, touchline – the lines at the side of the field of play. When they are touched by the ball or the player carrying it, the ball is said to be out.

Touch judge – the official on the touchline who signals when the ball is out.

Touchdown – a defender grounding the ball in his own in-goal area.

Touchline tackle – a tackle which pushes or drives the ball carrier over the touchline.

Try – the grounding of the ball by an attacking player in his opponent's in-goal area.

Unit – a small group of players working together.

Upright – one of the posts that make up the goalposts.

Up-and-under – a high kick to test or put pressure on the opposition (also called a Garryowen).

Wallabies – nickname for the Australian Rugby team.

Wheel – when a scrum moves through more than 90 degrees.

Willie-away – a peel from the lineout, named after All Black Wilson Whineray who was perhaps the first player to do the move.

Wing – the players closest to the touchlines (like the end of a bird's wing).

Wing-threequarters - wing.

Wipers kick – an angled kick across the field (like the angle of a windshield wiper).

Index

Useful Addresses

Associations, Leagues and Teams

International Rugby Board
Hugenot House
35-38 St Stephens Green
Dublin 2, Ireland
http://www.irfb.com
Founded in 1886, governing body encompasses 91 national rugby unions and one regional association. Member of the International Olympic Committee.
Publishes *Oval World* magazine.

Rugby Canada
National Sport and Recreation Centre
1600 James Naismith Drive
Gloucester, ON K1B 5N4
Tel: (613) 748-5657
Fax: (613) 748-5739
Web: http://www.rugbycanada.ca
More than 50,000 players in 211 clubs. Founded in 1929. Website has links to provincial clubs.

USA National Rugby Team
Hudson Rugby Fieldhouse
Berkeley, CA 94720-4426
Tel: (510) 643-1971
Fax: (510) 643-2192
Web: http://www.usa-eagles.org
United States' national team.

USA Rugby Football Union
3595 E. Fountain Blvd.
Colorado Springs, CO 80910
Tel: (719) 637-1022
Fax: (719) 637-1315
Email: info@usarugby.org
Web: http://www.usarugby.org
Over 30,000 players in 951 clubs. Founded in 1975. Website has links to regional unions and clubs.

Clothing

American Rugby Outfitters
1510 Midway Court E6
Elk Grove Village, IL 60007
Toll-Free 1-800-467-8429
Web: http://www.americanrugby.com

Clarkson Imports
624 Williams Avenue
Runnemede, NJ 08078-1246
Tel: (856) 933-3690
http://www.full-motion-net.com/clarkson

Lionheart Rugbywear
270 South West Marine Drive
Vancouver, BC V5X 2R5
Web: http://www3.bc.sympatico.ca/lionheartrugby

Optimum USA
5422 Kiam Street
Houston, TX 77007
Toll-Free 1-800-659-8037
Tel: (713) 869-5585
Fax: (713) 869-5586
Web: http://www.optimumusa.com

Rugby America, Ltd.
2625 South Spring Street
Springfield, IL 62704
Toll-Free 1-888-784-2964
Tel: (217) 793-7275
Fax: (217) 528-8604
Web: http://www.rugby2000.com

Rugby Designs Unlimited
P.O. Box 6796
Beaverton, OR 97007-0796
Toll-Free: 1-800-784-2901
Web: http://www.europa.com/rugby

Rugby Imports
885 Warren Avenue
East Providence, RI 02914
Toll-Free 1-800-431-4514
Tel: (401) 438-2727
Fax (4010) 438-8260
http://www.rugbyimports.com

Rugbywear
1704 St. James Street
Winnipeg, MB R3H 0L3
Tel: (204) 632-4222
Fax: (204) 694-8883
Web: http://www.rugbywear.com

Ruggers
591 Memorial Drive
Chicopee, MA 01020
Toll-Free: 1-877-784-4377
Tel: (413) 593-5503
Fax: (413) 593-1857
Web: http://www.ruggers.com

Publications

National Rugby Post
13228 - 76 Street
Edmonton, AB T5C 1B6
Tel: (780) 476-0268
Fax (780) 473-1066
Web: www.rugbypost.com

New Zealand Rugby News
PO Box 47125
Auckland, New Zealand
http://www.rugbynews.co.nz

Oval World
IRB Services (Ireland) Ltd
Hugenot House
35-38 St Stephens Green
Dublin 2, Ireland
Publication of the International Rugby Board.
Not available at retail.

Rugby
2350 Broadway
New York, NY 10024
Tel: (212) 787-1160
Fax: (212) 595-0934
Web: http://www.inch.com/~rugby

Rugby World
PO Box 272, Haywards Heath
West Sussex, RH16 3FS
England
Tel: +44 (162) 277-8778
Fax: +44 (144) 444-5599
Web: http://www.rugbyworld.com

Websites

http://www.onerugbyplace.com
http://planet-rugby.com
http://rugby365.com
http://www.rugbyguide.com
http://www.rugbyrugby.com
http://www.scrum.com
http://www.sports.com/rugby
http://www.usrl.com
http://www.worldofrugby.com